VICTIMOLOGY
The Victim and His Criminal

VICTIMOLOGY

The Victim and His Criminal

STEPHEN SCHAFER
Northwestern University

Reston Publishing Company, Inc., Reston, Virginia
A Prentice-Hall Company

Library of Congress Cataloging in Publication Data

Schafer, Stephen.
  Victimology : the victim and his criminal.

  Published in 1968 under title: The victim and his criminal.
  Bibliography: p.
  Includes indexes.
  1. Victims of crimes. 2. Reparation.
I. Title:
HV6250.25.S32 1977   364   76-26976
ISBN 0-87909-874-0
ISBN 0-87909-873-2 pbk.

© 1977 by Reston Publishing Company, Inc.
A Prentice-Hall Company
11480 Sunset Hills Road
Reston, Virginia 22090

10 9 8 7 6 5 4 3 2 1

Printed in the United States of America

To Eric

Contents

Preface

Victimology has come a long way towards being recognized as an integral and significant part of the etiology of crime. In addition to the ever-increasing number of studies in the area of criminal-victim relationships, there have been two international congresses devoted exclusively to victimology, and many national and international seminars and workshops have been organized to discuss the relationship between the victim and his criminal and to shed more light upon the victim's functional role in crime. And more and more universities are beginning to include a course in victimology in their curricula.

In less than a decade, so much attention has been paid to the victim of crime that the word *victim* has become subject to a "fashionable" usage. Often, unfortunately, it has been placed into a meaningless context, and its misuse may have misguided a not-too-

attentive audience. Some of those involved in problems of criminology have included the victim in their observations and en-
tangled him in their investigative efforts only to enhance the
popular appeal of their projects. Large scale and expensive "victimization" studies have been made that entirely missed the etymo-
logical point that *victimization* means not simply committing a
crime, but "making someone or something the victim of a criminal offense"; such studies, therefore, illuminate the criminal-victim *relationship* only thinly and in most cases only from a blurring
statistical distance, ending up as prosaic and ordinary crime
studies that have little to do with what victimology really entails.

This book was originally published under the title *The Victim
and His Criminal: A Study in Functional Responsibility.* This new
revised and enlarged edition, however, carries the title *Victimology:
The Criminal and His Victim* in order to put a heavier emphasis
on the conceptual scope of what is generally understood to be
victimology.

STEPHEN SCHAFER

VICTIMOLOGY
The Victim and His Criminal

Introduction

This book is an introduction to the study of criminal-victim relationships. This branch of learning has been called "victimology," but it is questionable whether denoting it as a specific doctrine or science is justified, or whether it should be considered as an integral part of the general crime problem.

"Victimology" is a new appellation, but it does not refer to a new idea: its importance has been recognized for centuries. Cesare Lombroso, in admitting to factors other than atavistic biological degeneration, considered that there were passionate criminals who acted under the pressure of victim-provoked emotions.[1] Raffaele Garofalo called attention to victim behaviors that could be regarded as provoking the offender to criminal action.[2] Enrico Ferri, in a somewhat indirect reference, mentioned those "pseudo-criminals" who violate the law because of the "inevitable necessity" of self-defense.[3] In his *Penal Philosophy*, Gabriel Tarde protested against

the "legislative mistake" of not considering motives indicative
of a significant interrelationship between victim and offender and
pointed out the possible responsibility of "some act of the victim's."[4]
August Goll presented a number of Shakespearean criminals whose
actions were motivated by their own victims;[5] and Josef Kohler
also referred to Shakespeare's dramas in describing victim-precipitated crimes that were committed "against the special nature"
(*contra naturam generis*) of the criminal.[6] Franz von Liszt, who
devoted so much of his life to the search for a comprehensive criminal typology, recognized the "self-preserving desperate" offenders
who act in response to insulted reputation, rejected love, shame, or
other victim-provoked emotional pressures;[7] and Ernst Seelig, too,
mentioned this type, naming them "crisis-criminals."[8]

The study of criminal-victim relationships, however, has always
suffered from a lack of organized imagination. The subject was
treated by early criminologists with only vague and oversimplified
allusions, which have not shed any clear light upon the nature of
the criminal-victim relationship. Although the field of victimology
has long been known, it has never developed from its embryonic
state and even now it has not evolved its dynamic possibilities.
Thus, this introduction to victimology can hardly attempt more
than a presentation of information about our limited knowledge,
mainly through the present responsibility concept of the criminal-
victim relationship, and, in the form of research results, some indications of future prospects for study.

Responsibility for one's conduct is a changing concept, and its
interpretation is a true mirror of the social, cultural, and political
conditions of the given era. Each developmental level in human
history is reflected in the contemporary laws, and the recognition
of criminal responsibility most often indicates the nature of societal
interrelationships and the ideology of the ruling power structure.
Who is responsible for what, and how, is defined by law; and law
is made by man. When the victim or his family began to demand
pecuniary compensation rather than the death of the offender, this
was due to a growing desire for the acquisition of private property,
outweighing the need for continuation of the perpetual blood-feud.
When the victim was deprived of his power to decide the penal
consequences of crime, this was due not only to the greed of feudal
barons who sought to gain the victim's share of compensation, but
also to the emergence of state criminal justice. When the Soviet

court practice tends to punish a murderer who committed his crime out of jealousy more severely then the offender of an ordinary homicide, this is not only a reproach for a worthless emotion, but also evidence of a certain disregard for the victim's responsibility for arousing a criminal passion.

The current interest in the criminal-victim relationship indicates that the understanding of crime has entered a new phase, and may mean the decline of the objective responsibility of the offender. There has been increasing recognition of the fact that criminal justice must consider the dynamics of crime and treat criminals as members of their total group—which includes the victim. The study of criminal-victim relationships emphasizes the need to recognize the role and responsibility of the victim, who is not simply the cause of and reason for the criminal procedure, but has a major part to play in the search for an objective criminal justice and a functional solution to the crime problem. Victimology also claims that the offender has responsibility for the reparation of any harm, injury, or other disadvantage caused to his victim.

In the structure of criminal law, *criminals* and *victims* refer to two distinct categories. However, as Hentig states, "experience tells us that this is not all, that the relationships between perpetrator and victim are much more intricate than the rough distinctions of criminal law." Doer and sufferer often appear in crime in a close interpersonal relationship where the victim may be one of the determinants of the criminal action. After the crime there is a minimal relationship; the doer stands far apart from the suffering of his victim. The "contribution of the victim to the genesis of crime"[10] and the contribution of the criminal to the reparation of his offense are the central problems of victimology. This, in essence, is the problem of responsibility. An immense volume of information has been accumulated about crime, but we have little knowledge about the criminal and even less about the victim and his connection to the crime and criminal. As stated in the Report of the President's National Crime Commission, "one of the most neglected subjects in the study of crime is its victims."[11]

Thus, this study could have other titles, and perhaps "*problems of the criminal-victim relationships*" would be more appropriate. This work does not assume to present the solution to the manifold problems of this field. Rather, it attempts to offer an orientation to victimology and to develop stimuli for further investigations.

NOTES

1. Gathered from several works of Cesare Lombroso, essentially from, *L'uomo delinquente* (5th ed., Torino, 1896), and *Delitti vecchi e delitti nuovi* (Torino, 1902).

2. Raffaele Garofalo, *Criminology,* trans. Robert Wyness Millar (Boston, 1914), p. 373.

3. Enrico Ferri, *Les Criminels dans l'art et la littérature,* French trans. Eugéne Laurent (Paris, 1902), p. 19.

4. Gabriel Tarde, *Penal Philosophy,* trans. R. Howell (Boston, 1912), p. 466.

5. August Goll, *Verbrecher bei Shakespeare,* German trans. Oswald Gerloff (Stuttgart, c. 1908).

6. Josef Kohler, *Verbrecher-Typen in Shakespeares Dramen* (Berlin, c. 1905).

7. Franz von Liszt, *Strafrechtliche Aufsätze und Vorträge* (Berlin, 1905).

8. Ernst Seelig, "Die Gliederung der Verbrecher," in Ernst Seelig and Karl Weindler, eds., *Die Typen der Kriminellen* (Berlin, 1949), p. 6.

9. Hans von Hentig, *The Criminal and His Victim, Studies in the Sociobiology of Crime* (New Haven, 1948), p. 383.

10. Ibid.

11. *The Challenge of Crime in a Free Society,* Report of the President's Commission on Law Enforcement and Administration of Justice, U.S. Government Printing Office, Washington, D.C., February 1967, p. 38.

1

The History of the Victim

The Golden Age of the Victim

The only aspect of the criminal-victim relationship that has been
recognized throughout history is the harm, injury, or other damage
caused by the criminal to his victim. Until recently there has been
virtually no consideration of the victim's participation in the wrongdoing, or of any other interaction or interrelationship between
criminal and victim. The term "golden age" of the victim refers to
the time during which there was recognition of the victim's important role and an emphasis on compensation. The historical origin
of the victim's dominant role in criminal procedure lies in the
Middle Ages and is plainly evident in the system of "composition"
(compensation) in the Germanic common laws.[1]

The Victim's Role in Social Control

We can refer to the Middle Ages as the common past of compensation and punishment. A common past does not, of course, imply a common present or future, but neither the adherents nor the opponents of victim-compensation can be indifferent to the fact that restitution to victims of crime is an ancient institution that for a long period was almost inseparably attached to the institution of punishment.

The basis of primitive and early Western law was personal reparation by the offender or the offender's family to the victim. When political institutions were largely based upon kinship ties or tribal organization, and when there was an absence of a central authority to determine guilt and the kind of punishment, some forms of revenge, blood-feud, vendetta, or pecuniary compensation were common practices.[2]

In the earliest history of mankind, social control was in the hands of the individual—primitive man—who was alone in his struggle for existence. Alone, he faced attacks from outside and fought against fellow creatures who caused him harm. He had to take the law into his own hands; in effect, he made the law, and he was the victim, the prosecutor, and the judge. He carried out the punishment in the form of revenge aimed at deterrence and compensation. It was a private revenge and the compensation was exclusively personal.

In that primitive period the criminal-victim relationship mirrored the struggle for survival. It was probably not the idea of responsibility, but rather the security of his "social" power and the prevention of future crimes that guided the victim to ruthless retaliation and aggressively acquired compensation. Attack was the defense against attack, and the state of war between the criminal and his victim made the sufferer a doer and converted criminals to victims. The criminal-victim relationship at that time was hardly anything more than a mutually opposed effort to secure power.

When the first primitive groups were firmly established, the social control was maintained by the kindred (this, and not the bloody nature of revenge, explains the word "blood" in the term "blood-feud"), and there was need for neither suprafamilial authority nor for state control. Even among highly organized hunters, such as the Cheyenne and the Comanches, tribal law was all that was necessary. An offense against the individual was an offense against his clan or tribe, and although the punishment to be exacted from the offender was neither codified nor always standardized by offense, some form of restitution or compensation was invariably involved in the interrelationship between the victim and offender. In this respect, the individual victim's position was very often taken over by his whole clan or tribe, and the offender's position was likewise projected to his whole family. An individual did not punish another individual; families took revenge on families. This can be considered the origin of the concept of collective responsibility, which has emerged again in the twentieth century and has resulted in the death of millions.

Injury to the person was scaled in accordance with the seriousness of the trespass and the social evaluation of the aggrieved party. Typically, as among the Ifugoa in Northern Luzon, the determination of damages involved five critical factors: the nature of the offense, the relative class positions of the litigants, the solidarity and behavior of the two kinship groups involved in the dispute, the personal tempers and reputations of the two principals, and the geographical position of the two kin groups. There were traditional scales of damages for various offenses, and because of the property and money orientation of the culture, some punitive damages were pecuniary. For instance, in the case of the rape of a married woman by a married man, both her own and her husband's kin groups were offended. Each collected damages equivalent to those paid in the case of aggravated adultery. If the rapist were married, he paid these damages not only to the woman's and her husband's, but also to his wife's kin.[3]

This blood-revenge was still a part of the struggle for survival: a safeguard to the victim for the preservation of all potentials for existence, by means of unlimited aggression, if necessary.[4] In addition to comparatively minor crimes within the tribe or clan, the important crime type of this era consisted of external threats to one tribe or family by another. Punishment for some crimes was achieved by a form of compensation or restitution, but most punishment was through aggressive retaliation. As if it were the scene of our modern international world, both criminal (one tribe) and victim (another tribe) wanted to weaken or exterminate each other: "crime" was the violation of the tribal "international law." The blood-revenge tested the relations among families.

The blood-feud might have been a precursor of the responsibility laws, but since it was informal and had no defined conditions it cannot be regarded as a social institution. As Rudolf Ihering put it, "all laws started with arbitrariness and revenge."[5] Regardless of reality, the judgment of whether or not an act was a crime was entirely dependent upon the victim's arbitrary assumption. The blood-revenge had to be justified in order to intensify the clan members' determination to exact an aggressive retribution. In spite of its strong resemblance to punishment, the blood-feud served an unromantic and vital interest: the tribe, clan, or family could continue living and functioning only if its strength and power remained intact and efficient enough to repulse dangerous attacks. Thus, blood-revenge was aimed essentially at the restoration of the balance of power in the world of primitive societies. At this developmental stage of history, such punishment was not really a response to the criminal's "product-responsibility," but was an expression of social defense. The attacker and his family were held responsible for endangering the existence of the attacked tribe, rather than for the "product" (that is, the actual objective result) of the attack.

As the material culture reached a higher level of development and included a richer inventory of economic goods, a threat to these goods came to be equated with physical or mental hurt. Thus, a trend toward composition is a noticeable corollary of the social and economic evolution.[6]

Early references to compensation are sporadic and do not offer clear information.[7] The death fine in Greece is referred to more than once in Homer:[8] in the Ninth Book of the Iliad, Ajax, in reproaching Achilles for not accepting Agamemnon's offer of reparation, reminds him that even a brother's death may be appeased by a pecuniary fine, and that the murderer, having paid the fine, may remain at home free among his own people. Not only in the time of the Greeks, but in still earlier ages, when the Mosaic Dispensation was established among the Hebrews, traces of restitution to the victim are apparent. "That Dispensation, in its penal department, took special and prominent cognizance of the rights and claims of the injured persons, as against the offender."[9] For example, if two men were involved in a fight and one hit the other with a stone or with his fist with the result that the opponent was badly injured but did not die, the perpetrator was required to pay for the loss of the injured man's time and to cause him to be thoroughly healed.[10]

For injuries both to person and property, restitution or reparation in some form was the chief and often the only element of punishment. Among Semitic nations the death fine was general practice and it continued to prevail in the Turkish Empire.[11]

Indian Hinduism required restitution and atonement: He who stones is forgiven. In the Sutra period in India the settling of compensation was treated as a royal right: for murder the offender was obliged by the king to compensate the relatives of the deceased or the king or both. In the time of Manu, compensation was regarded as a penance: hence it might be owed to the priests. Islam also enjoins restitution and atonement.[12]

In addition to these sources, the Law of Moses, which required fourfold restitution for stolen sheep and fivefold for the more useful ox,[13] and the Code of Hammurabi (formulated about 2200 B.C.), which was notorious for its deterrent cruelty, sometimes demanding even thirty times the value of the damage caused, suggest that the criminal's obligation to pay was enforced not in the interest of the victim, but rather for the purpose of increasing the severity of the criminal's punishment. Where the offender against society paid for his crimes with "an eye for an eye, a tooth for a tooth," he paid as an object of the victim's vengeance, not in compensation for the victim's injury. Individual compensation, if any, was largely related to property damage and generally did not apply to personal injuries.[14]

The Code of Hammurabi was a combination of civil and criminal stipulations presented in an unorganized fashion. It was much less sophisticated than the jurisprudence of the Roman law, and emphasized the idea of deterrence not only through the cruel severity of the penal consequences, but also by keeping alive the collective responsibility of the family. For instance, in case of a theft (as seen in articles 22–24), if the thief escaped, everyone in his home town was responsible to the victim, even those who did not know about the crime. The trend toward composition developed parallel with the strong remnants of the blood-revenge of families against families.

In spite of the fairly close relationship between the ancient Roman criminal and civil law, it is not easy to find reliable information concerning the position of the victim or restitution to him. According to the Law of the Twelve Tables, a thief who was caught in the act of committing the theft was obliged to pay double the value of the stolen object. In cases where the stolen object was found in a search of his house, he was to pay three times the value, or four times the value if he resisted the execution of the house search. He was to pay four times the value of the object if he had stolen it by force or threat of violence. In certain cases the kinship was exposed to the revenge of the victim.

In the case of slander, also, the insulting person had to pay. The sum to be paid was decided by the magistrate according to the rank of the victim, his relation to the offender, the seriousness of the offense, and the place it was committed. Generally, in case of any *delictum* or *quasi delictum* the offender was obliged to pay damages, and in exceptional cases the specially assessed value of the article damaged or lost as well.

Despite these requirements, the 48th and 49th Books of the Digest (*libri terribiles*) do not contain any clear reference to the consideration of the victim's role in the case or to restitution or compensation. There are some vague passages that indicate a presumption that in certain cases the judge might consider the civil claim within the scope of the criminal procedure.[15] In any case, while the history of Roman law shows some general decline from its classic stage to the Justinian period, its system of responsibility reached a higher level than any other previous law.

Because of the increasing importance of economic goods the delictual conditions started to change and the system of responsibility was transformed: blood-feud faded out and physical retribution began to be replaced by financial compensation. The criminal and his victim introduced the redemption of revenge (in its original German, *Loskauf der Rache*) and submitted the judgment of guilt to negotiation. In most cases, the agreement on the question of compensation still involved both interested political entities—the criminal's tribe, clan, or family and that of the victim. It took some time until the individual offender and the individual victim stood somewhat as they had in the era of private revenge, and negotiated guilt and punishment as two individuals.

However, it was only toward the end of the Middle Ages that the concept of restitution was closely related to that of punishment, and was temporarily included in penal law.[16] Still, the victim's role in the crime itself was not considered at all, and his participation in criminal procedure served only to gain satisfaction for his injury. For example, under several systems in early American law, a thief, in addition to his punishment, was ordered to return three times the value of the stolen goods, or, in the case of insolvency, to place his person at the disposal of the victim for a certain length of time.[17] In the Germanic common laws a further refinement transformed retaliation into the system of composition; even murder could be compensated for between the wrongdoer and the nearest relative of the slain.[18] The "law of injury" seems to have been ruled by the idea of reciprocity.[19]

"Composition," the Medieval Tariff of the Victim

The change from vengeful retaliation to composition was part of a natural historical process. As tribes settled down, reaction to injury or loss became less severe. Compensation to the victim (the composition) served to mitigate blood-feuds, which, as tribes became more or less stable communities, only caused endless trouble because an injury would start a perpetual vendetta.[20] Composition offered an alternative that was in many ways equally satisfactory to the victim. In Arabia, Tyler noted, the tribes outside the cities usually adhered strictly to the blood-feud, but tribes in the cities found it necessary to practice compensation for offenses against the person in order to prevent the socially disintegrating effects of the blood-feud.[21] Among German tribes, the criminal was humiliated to some extent by compensation, which appeased the victim's desire for revenge.[22] At this time it was assumed that the victim should seek revenge or satisfaction; this was the only aspect of the criminal-victim relationship that gained recognition. Among the ancient Germans, said Tacitus, "even homicide is atoned by a certain fine in cattle and sheep; and the whole family accepts the satisfaction to the advantage of the public weal, since quarrels are most dangerous in a free state."[23]

Composition combined punishment with damages. For this reason it could be applied only to personal wrongs, not to public crimes.[24] This was also why, in its first stage of development, it was subject to private compromise. This supports the view that during the Middle Ages the penal law of communities, in which crimes were paid for by restitution, was not a law of crimes, but a law of torts.[25] Thus, criminal-victim relationships could be viewed only in terms of the victim's revengeful emotions and his claim for compensation. The injuring party offered monetary satisfaction or something else of economic value. If the injured party accepted it, he was fully revenged and the "criminal procedure" was complete.

Payment was made entirely to the victim or his family. The amount depended on the importance and extent of the injury. The Germanic common laws were objective: composition was determined by the effect of the wrongful act, and not by the offender's subjective guilt. This was no longer an expression of social defense, but a response to the criminal's "product-responsibility." Neither the general security interest of the tribe or family nor the criminal intent or individual guilt of the offender decided the range of composition. It was decided by the "crime-product." In other words, the objective result of the offense served as the victim's most important guide for the judgment of the criminal.

The amount of compensation varied according to the nature of the crime and the age, rank, sex, and prestige of the injured party: "A free-born man is worth more than a slave, a grown-up more than a child, a man more than a woman, and a person of rank more than a freeman."[26] Thus, the "value" of human beings and their social positions were involved in determining compensation, and a socially stratified composition developed. By the time of Alfred in 871, the feud was resorted to only after compensation had been requested and refused. The "Dooms of Alfred" provided that if a man knocked out the front teeth of another man, he was to pay him eight shillings; if it was an eye tooth, four shillings; if a molar, fifteen shillings. These dooms detailed the compensation for a variety of crimes against the person.[27]

It is difficult to pinpoint the start of new developments in community judicial control, since the community traditionally exercised a certain collective control over the extent of compensation. The bridge to state criminal law had as a support the system of composition, and the settlement by periodical tribal assemblies of the amount to be paid provides an early example of judicial proceedings. Soon after the emergence of composition, some laws (*leges barbarorum*) elaborated an intricate system of compensation. Every kind of blow or wound given to every kind of person had its price.[28] From the many differences in the amount of damages and in the "value" of the victim, a complicated system of regulations evolved that dominated the earliest codified law of many peoples, particularly that of the Anglo-Saxons.[29] Several aspects of the laws of Aethelred and of Alfred are mentioned by Clarence R. Jeffery: "Henceforth, if anyone slay a man, he shall himself bear the vendetta, unless with the help of his friends he pay compensation for it within twelve months to the full amount of the slain man's *wergeld,* according to the inherited rank. . . . The authorities must put a stop to the vendettas. First, according to the public, the slayer shall give security to his advocate and the advocate to the kinsmen of the slain man, that he, the slayer, will make reparation to the kindred. . . . If a man has a spear over his shoulder, and anyone is transfixed thereon, he shall pay the *wergeld* without the fine. If a bone is laid bare, 3 shillings shall be paid as compensation. If a shoulder is disabled, 30 shillings shall be as compensation."[30]

Presumably *Friedlosigkeit,* and in other places outlawry, which resulted from a failure to provide composition, developed in connection with these tariff regulations. If the wrongdoer was reluctant to pay or could not pay the necessary sum, he was declared a *friedlos* or outlaw: he was to be ostracized, and anybody might kill him with impunity.[31]

Some Longobard laws openly declared the principle that it was necessary to put a more accurate financial value on individuals.[32] Punishment, reparation, restitution, compensation—all were represented and unified in the composition in accordance with the value of the injured person. The place of the victim on the scale of money values was of the greatest importance to the criminal: since the amount of composition was determined by assessing his victim, the criminal could tell whether or not he could pay the amount demanded. Obviously, a low assessment was in his interest, but he could do little about it, since the victim was evaluated by his community. The criminal's risk was extreme. Loss of membership in his group meant, in fact, the loss of existence. Alone, he could do nothing to obtain the necessities of life. Moreover, he lost the protection provided by his community. Alone, he could not defend himself against the revenge of others. He could continue a meaningful and safe existence only if he paid the amount equated with the value of his victim.

However, the influence of state power over composition gradually increased. As a result, the criminal's position was somewhat eased. *Friedlosigkeit* stopped being a necessary consequence of an unsatisfied compositional demand. The community claimed a share of the victim's compensation, and as the central power in a community grew stronger its share increased.

A share is claimed by the community or overlord or king as a commission for its trouble in bringing about a reconciliation between the parties, or, perhaps, as the price payable by the malefactor either for the opportunity that the community secures for him of redeeming his wrong by a money payment, or for the protection that it affords him, after he has satisfied the award, against further retaliation on the part of the man whom he has injured.[33]

One part of the composition went to the victim (*Wergeld, Busse, emenda, lendis*). The other part went to the community or the king (*Friedensgeld, fredus, gewedde*).[34] In Saxon England, the *Wer,* or payment for homicide, and the *Bot,* the betterment[35] or compensation for injury, existed alongside the *Wite,* or fine paid to the king or overlord.[36]

This twofold payment enabled the offender to buy back the security that he had lost. The double nature of the payment shows clearly the close connection between punishment and compensation.[37]

Before long the injured person's right to restitution began to shrink, and, after the Treaty of Verdun divided the Frankish Empire, the fine that went to the state gradually replaced it entirely. The double payment continued, but now the king or overlord took all of it. Discretionary money penalties took the place of the old *wites,* while the *bot* gave way to damages, assessed by a tribunal.[38] As the state monopolized the institution of punishment,[39] the rights of the injured were slowly separated from the penal law: composition, as the obligation to pay damages, became separated from criminal law and became a special field in civil law.[40]

With this development, the "golden age" of the victim came to an end. It had been an era when his possible participation in any wrongdoing was not taken into consideration. During that time, in fact, it seems inconceivable that the victim's relationship with the criminal could have helped to develop or precipitate the crime. The criminal-victim relationship was strictly divided between the active role of the doer and the passive role of the sufferer. The criminal alone was responsible for the crime. The victim was merely the injured party; he was not thought to be involved in any psychological intricacies of crime causation, and pushed his every advantage as the object of a crime that was allegedly caused only by the criminal. He had almost dictatorial power over the settlement of the criminal case; at no other time in the history of crime has the victim occupied such an advantageous position in criminal procedure.

This state of affairs marks the closing phase of the centuries-long period during which criminal procedure was the private or personal concern of the victim or his family and was largely under their control. The injury, harm, or other wrong done to the victim was not only the main or essential issue of the criminal case; it was the only issue. In the criminal procedure there was no room for societal or other considerations. The survival and power of the group, so often the real reason behind the criminal procedure, remained almost always behind the scenes. The procedure was exclusively aimed at the private compensation of the victim, which took the form of private revenge (or private blood-vengeance) or private composition. (Compensation was a form of punishment or revenge and should not be confused with bribes that were given to avoid criminal proceedings. Bribes as "blood money" are an entirely different matter and have been known throughout history. For example, Demosthenes (384?–322 B.C.) mentions in his speech "Against Pantainetos" (58.28–29) that Theokrines made a bargain with his brother's murderer instead of starting legal proceedings against him). It did not require social sanction, and was nobody else's business. One of the few social obligations that developed from this system can be traced to ancient Athens, where it was the duty of the family to obtain vengeance or retribution and "to fail to take action was a disgrace." But even here the victim was in fact the only master of "criminal justice," to the extent that a dying murder victim would sometimes instruct his family to take revenge.[41]

It was indeed the golden age of the victim. Criminal justice served only his private interests. No other aspects of crime could compete with this concept in this privately owned and privately administered criminal law.

The Decline of the Victim

Feudal Barons and Ecclesiastical Powers

"It was chiefly owing to the violent greed of feudal barons and medieval ecclesiastical powers that the rights of the injured party were gradually infringed upon, and finally to a large extent, appropriated by these authorities, who exacted a double vengeance, indeed, upon the offender, by forfeiting his property to themselves instead of to his victim, and then punishing him by the dungeon, the torture, the stake or the gibbet. But the original victim of wrong was practically ignored."[42]

After the Middle Ages, restitution, as a concept separate from punishment, seems to have been on the wane. Little as we know about crime today, even less was known then. No other possible aspect of the victim's role was taken into consideration, and the victim became the "poor relation" of the criminal law.[43]

The decline in the penological importance of restitution and non-recognition of the victim's functional role in crime gained theoretical support from the endeavor to find different bases for penal and civil liability.

Voigt distinguished between the provisions of the Law of the Twelve Tables according to the object of their sanctions: if a sanction was stipulated against the person, he regarded it as part of the criminal law, but if a sanction was directed against property, he listed it in the body of civil law.[44] Josef Kohler and Ziehbart regarded all Greek responsibility laws as belonging to penal law if the responsible person had to provide reparation to the injured individual as well as to the state.[45] Mommsen realized the great difficulties in distinguishing between criminal and civil law, and attempted to do so by pointing out that moral duties, if prescribed by the state, are parts of penal law; however, the confusing relationship between reparative and retributive sanctions prompted him to make a further distinction between public (*öffentliches*) and private (*privates*) criminal laws.[46]

The multiplicity of other theories that distinguished between civil and penal liability revealed two trends. According to the subjective view, penal liability results from deliberate infringement of the law. It differs from civil liability in that the latter does not involve strong deliberate opposition to the will of the state. (This theory fails to take into account criminal offenses committed through negligence. On the other hand, there are certain kinds of deliberate infringement that give rise to civil liability only).

According to the objective view, however, penal wrong involves a direct injury to the victim, which exists in and of itself, apart from any statement made by the victim. This differs from civil illegality, which is an indirect injury solely dependent on the victim's statement. (This theory fails to consider that infringement of the civil law can exist independently of the statement of the victim. On the other hand, *volenti non fit injuria* has some application to criminal law).

Generally speaking, since the era of composition, the conventional view is that a crime is an offense against the state, while a tort is an offense only against individual rights.[47] Also, in accordance with this thinking, crime means only the offender and his offense; the victim's relationship to the crime is viewed in a civil rather than in a criminal light.

However this may be, the system of composition surrendered only after a struggle; even after the German-Busse penal law there are records of victims who, in spite of the common law character of the criminal law, asked for indemnification and personal satisfaction as well as public punishment. The connection between crime and restitution (*continentia causae*) might have lessened, but could not be completely disregarded, even after the introduction of the procedure of inquisition, in which the theoretical and practical distinctions between the demands of penal law and those of the victim are most acute. Court practice in the sixteenth and seventeenth centuries (*Gerichtspraxis des gemeinen Rechts*) made possible the so-called *adhesive procedure* (*Adhäsionprozess*), which opened the way for discretion by a court, concerning the victim's claim for restitution, within the scope of the criminal proceedings.[48] Penal codes of the nineteenth century also seemed to give some support to the idea of restitution in the form of the adhesive procedure. This procedure appears in about half the laws of the federal German states. Later on, however, the situation got worse, and even in the German law of criminal procedure, the idea of restitution was kept alive only by the force of tradition.[49]

The Victim's Case on the International Scene

Advocates of restitution and defenders of the victim's role in the judgment of crime did not look on with folded arms; they could not accept the deterioration of the victim's position. They thought of the victim's problem only in relation to his compensation and as if he had made no contribution to the crime itself. In 1847 Bonneville de Marsangy outlined a plan of reparation,[50] and later on, several international prison or penitentiary congresses enthusiastically advocated reestablishing the rights of victims of crime.

At the International Prison Congress held in Stockholm in 1878, Sir George Arney, Chief Justice of New Zealand, and William Tallack proposed a general return to the ancient practice of making reparation to the injured.[51] Raffaele Garofalo raised the question at the International Prison Congress held in Rome in 1885[52] and wrote that reparation to the victim is "a matter of justice and social security."[53] The problem was also discussed at the International Prison Congress held at St. Petersburg in 1890 and at the International Penal Association Congress held at Christiania in 1891. At this congress the following conclusions were adopted:

1. Modern law does not sufficiently consider the reparation due to injured parties.
2. In the case of petty offense, time should be given for indemnification.
3. Prisoners' earnings in prison might be utilized for this end.

The problem of victim compensation was exhaustively discussed at the International Prison Congress held in Paris in 1895. This was the last of quinquennial series and was attended by penologists such as France's Bérenger, Bertillon, Bonneville de Marsangy, Tarde, Vidal; Germany's Krohne and Mittermaier; Russia's Foinitsky; Italy's Beltrany-Scalia and Garofalo; Belgium's Prins; the Netherland's Van Hamel; Switzerland's Guillaume. Question 4 of Section I of the Agenda asked: "Is the victim of a delict sufficiently armed by modern law to enable him to obtain indemnity from the man who has injured him?"

At this congress it was felt that modern laws were particularly weak on victim compensation and that, in some respects, the laws of certain countries were harder on the victim than on the offender. The Italian penologists in particular had long urged that this matter be discussed, and Garofalo and Pierantoni dealt with it in an impressive manner. It was also the subject of valuable papers by Cornet, Flandin, Pascaud, Poet, Prins, and Zucker. These papers insisted that compensation or restitution should be made by offenders to the persons they had injured. The final resolutions of the Paris congress were similar in principle to those made in 1891 at Christiania, but it was decided, "in the absence of sufficient evidence," to express no conclusion. The problem was earmarked for further discussion, however, and was duly included in the agenda of the next prison congress, the Sixth International Penitentiary Congress, held at Brussels in 1900. Section I of Question 1 was: "What would be, following the order of ideas indicated by the Congress of Paris, the most practical means of securing for the victim of a criminal offense the indemnity due him from the delinquent?" The problem of restitution again became the subject of exhaustive discussion by the most respected penologists of the time.

The *rapporteur* of the question, the Belgian representative, Adolphe Prins, pressed for a decisive vote. The matter, he reminded the delegates, had been discussed in successive congresses with zeal and almost with passion for fifteen years. The congress, however, came no nearer to a solution of the problem than the Paris congress. It did no more than reaffirm a resolution made in Paris in favor of a reform of procedure that would facilitate civil action.[54]

At the turn of the century the victim's case continued to be advanced, but without success. Were there any promising signs on the horizon? This matter will be discussed in the section on the revival of the importance of the victim.

The Type of Society and Its Victim

It has frequently been noted that the separation of civil and penal functions is a serious defect in the system of fines, which go only to the state, while the injured victim suffers all the hardships of the civil process. However, except for sporadic efforts, there is still a tendency to move the question of compensation or restitution more and more out of criminal procedure, palpably in the desire to keep the victim from being involved in it.[55] The victim, so the argument runs, should not be interested financially in the outcome of the prosecution; he should not be interested in it at all, and concern for the victim should not disturb crimino-political purposes.[56] The argument clearly indicates that the victim is not accepted as an important role player in crime. History suggests that growing interest in the reformation of the criminal is matched by decreasing care for and interest in the victim.

And the victim is continuing to lose ground: if one examines the legal systems of different countries, one rarely finds an instance in which the victim of a crime can be certain to expect full restitution.

Similarly, hardly any legal systems take fully into consideration the victim's contribution to a crime. In those rare cases where there is state compensation, the system either is not fully effective or does not work at all. Where there is no system of state compensation, civil procedure and civil execution generally offer the victim insufficient compensation.[57] While the punishment of crime is regarded as the concern of the state, the injurious result of the crime —that is to say, the wrong or damage to the victim—is regarded almost as a private matter. It recalls the lonely man of the early days of social development, who by himself had to find compensation, and who by himself had to take revenge against those who harmed or otherwise wronged him. Today's victim cannot seek satisfaction on his own, since his state forbids him to take the law into his own hands. At the same time, though, the state is not concerned with his precipitative or causative part in the criminal offense.

We may assume that the number of victims has increased at the same rate as the number of criminals, if not at a higher rate. But even this fact has failed to halt the weakening of the victim's position; there has been no improvement in the victim's lot to compare with the advances that have been made in criminology, and certainly no improvement to compare with the amelioration of the criminal's lot. Criminal law is considered primitive among people living at a low cultural level, not because criminal justice is practiced by the victim himself as a recompense for his injury, but because the group or state takes no part in it, and because there is no agency of social control against crime. However, ever since the state took over from the victim the task of preserving law and order and keeping the peace, concern for its predecessor (that is, the victim) in administering criminal justice has been lacking. "It is rather absurd that the state undertakes to protect the public against crime and then, when a loss occurs, takes the entire payment and offers no effective remedy to the individual victim."[58] Perhaps it is similarly absurd that, whenever a crime occurs, the entire blame is placed on the offender without taking a dynamic view of the crime from every angle, and without considering, among other things, any precipitative or causative behavior by the victim that may have eventually affected the development or concept of the crime. Criminal responsibility has become one-directional.

The golden age of the victim was a part of the *Gemeinschaft-*

type social structure, where social relations were familistic, involuntary, primary, sacred, traditional, emotional, personal; but the lessening of the victim's role was a result of the development, to use Tönnies' terminology,[59] of the contractual *Gesellschaft* system, characterized by social interaction that is voluntary, secular, secondary, rationalistic, impersonal.[60] Private or family vengeance was replaced by social retribution, and the retaliatory rationale of punishment became socialized; even the continued use of the death penalty may in part be due to this legal and psychological transference from the idea of compensation for the victim or the victim's family to the idea of social revenge for a crime involving total loss to the individual.[61] "One of the fundamental differences between modern and traditional society," Robert A. Nisbet points out, "is the degree of legal and moral autonomy possessed by individuals."[62]

The history of the politically organized legal order is, in fact, not much different from the history of criminal responsibility and is most closely connected with the history of the victim. When social revenge replaced private revenge or the blood-feud, and the socially controlled judicial administration of law removed the maintenance of the social order from individuals or familial groups, this reflected developing changes in the understanding of responsibility and the position of the victim. It was characteristic of the *Gemeinschaft*-type social structure that the personal relationship of the criminal with his victim was not a necessary part of the "criminal justice"; not only because the criminal-victim relationship in no way influenced the judgment, but primarily because what motivated a criminal did not affect his responsibility. As for judging, criminal conduct, victimization, punishment, damages—everything was impersonal. Also, responsibility had no personal point of reference; most often the direct recipient of the penal sanction had no *causal nexa* with the injury or other harm resulting from the crime. It is a long way from this undifferentiated product-responsibility to responsibility based on differentiated guilt; and even if the modern law against genocide reminds the superficial observer of the understanding of crime in a *Gemeinschaft*-style (in fact, genocide is a crime against humanity, rather than simply an existential attack against a familial group), only a differentiated guilt can actually lead to punishment.

Responsibility laws and the position of the victim are different in the *Gemeinschaft*-type society from those in the *Gesellschaft*-type social structure, because in the latter the definitions of crime and responsibility are for the protection of a given social order, its conditions, values, and interests. The system of responsibilities may be taken as a criminal- and victim-selecting strategy that reflects the philosophy and ideology of the given culture.

While the "private criminal law" was marked by the almost exclusive and dominant role of the victim, in the criminal law of the normative and organized social structure the victim became almost entirely excluded from the settlement of the criminal case. In contrast to the understanding of crime as a violation of the victim's interest, the emergence of the state developed another interpretation: the disturbance of the society. As a result, "the unfortunate victim of criminality is habitually ignored."[63] While the punishment of crime was regarded as the concern of the state and thus received more and more official and public support, the crime, as a wrong to the victim, came to be regarded as a private matter and from this viewpoint elicited little official or public concern. The state became interested only in the responsibility of the offender; this made the responsibility one-directional.

However, the decline of the victim's importance and the almost total neglect he suffered did not mean that he was placed completely outside criminal procedure. But his participation in the proceedings was reduced to an evaluation of the wrong that had been done to him. The particular wrong indicated the degree of seriousness of the crime. When the victim lost his control over the fate of the criminal and the state obtained the monopoly for conducting criminal procedure, the state administered justice only in the name of society and did not consider all functional social forces and the full dynamics of crime. The victim continued to be the "cause" of or "reason" for criminal procedure. Although he had no way of intervening in the outcome of the proceedings, had no right to take revenge or compensation, and did not risk involvement in the responsibility for the crime, *formally* the criminal procedure was and still is operated to protect the victim's individual right to his safety and integrity. The punishment is concerned with the individual guilt of the offender and is meted out in accordance with the particular wrong done to the individual victim.

This individualistic understanding of the crime problem was, at least when it was fully developed, a product of the eighteenth century. And although at that time this was a revolutionary change from the medieval arbitrariness of the judges, it deprived the victim of his power, rights, and potential value in helping criminal justice. In the individualistic era man demanded the right to pursue his own ends, to act independently, and to have his individuality respected by all. Criminal justice, although formally in compliance with this, was ready to see the criminal act as largely isolated from social problems. However, it was also ready to see it from the viewpoint of the victim's interest. Justice started to intervene with formalistic and rather bureaucratic legal thinking. Communal ideas and interests became abstractions no longer based on individual interests.

In this system, in which criminal law came to be overloaded with formal safeguards to individual freedom, one might have expected to see a well-integrated participation by the victim, in terms both of his compensation and of a recognition of his share in a crime; and if this was not built into the formalistic-individualistic structure, it might have been due to the state's exclusive possession and control of criminal justice. There must be more than a germ of truth in the suggestion that the medieval composition helped give rise to state criminal law but soon was emasculated by its own extreme individualization. The individualistic state criminal law proved to be particularistic only in viewing the criminal as an independent individual, in safeguarding the offender's individual rights, and in judging his crime as if it were merely an attack of one individual upon another. It was individualistic in inflicting punishment because of the injury to an individual victim and in proportion to the individual injury; but it ceased to be individualistic when it came to the individual interests and individual responsibilities of the victim.

The Revival of the Victim

Crime, against which the state undertakes the protection of the public, is a disturbance of some legally protected interest: usually an interest that the state safeguards because in the given social structure and value system current thought considers such an interest worthy of protection through punishment of anyone who violates it. Almost all crimes, perhaps aside from political offenses and others that are not material, involve an injury—physical, financial, or moral—done by one individual to another. This disturbance of a legally protected interest is regarded as a crime, that is to say, a criminal violation of law and order. The violator of public order is also an offender against an individual victim. There has been renewed recognition during the past few decades that crime gives rise to legal, moral, ethical, and psychic ties not only between the violator and society, but also between the violator and his victim. Crime upsets the balance not only between the criminal and his social group, but also between the criminal and the individual victim. Moreover, this upset may develop because of the criminal-victim relationship. In other words, a unitary view of crime requires that the victim again be included in an understanding of criminal deviations, both as one injured by the crime and as a participant in it.

This renewed recognition of the victim's role in the crime problem, or better, the beginning of his return to importance, is probably one of the signals heralding the decline of the formalistic-individualistic orientation in criminal law, which opens the way to the universalistic understanding of crime. In past centuries justice was exercised in the name of society, but only the harm or injury to the individual victim was emphasized, and punishment was meted out in accordance with the degree of the wrong. In the universalistic orientation of criminal law, on the other hand, the normative organization and value structure of the society in which the criminal and his victim live—and their relationship to this organization and to other members of their group—are beginning to determine the general perspective of the crime problem. Universalistic criminal law and criminology direct attention to what we tentatively call the criminal's—and perhaps also the victim's—"functional responsibility," rather than to isolated criminal action or conduct.[64]

The universalistic approach to the crime problem apparently has grown out of a recognition that the individualistic orientation might have favorable aspects, but leads only to social confusion. The result has often been stiff, static, and formalistic judgments, which take only a narrow view of the crime. The revival of the victim's importance includes the concept of viewing him and his offender as social phenomena that can be understood only through their relations to their social environment and to each other.

The individualistic criminal law can pride itself on the lasting achievement of having developed safeguards for, and protection of, the rights of the individual against the arbitrariness of the courts. But one of its shortcomings is that its statute books do not sufficiently take into account the variations of human interactions. It introduced abstraction as a dominating force, it introduced the rule of the paper, and it made criminal justice merely the interpretative machinery of the printed law: the goddess Justinia probably was impartial and knew the law very well, but her blindfold deprived her of the sight of complex interactions, group characteristics, and social problems. The criminal-victim relationship, like many other aspects of crime, therefore remained unknown to her.

The universalistic orientation of criminal law and criminology struggles against this lack of knowledge, and attempts to find a way to a more complete understanding of crime. It is not aimed at having the individual dissolved again in a sea of collectivity; nor is a universalistic approach to the crime problem intended to make the individual a medium of antiindividualistic goals. However, it does propose a revision of the classic concept of isolated individual guilt, and it proposes a stronger emphasis on the broader and more extensive concept of a functional responsibility.

Suprauniversalistic Orientation—the Modern Tariff of the Victim

The merit of a broader concept of criminal responsibility is strongly spelled out by the totalitarian interpretation of the universalistic orientation. This might be called the *suprauniversalistic* interpretation of the crime problem. In this interpretation a social (or, better, political) idea stands above not only individual interests, but also the conventional group interests of the society (interests of the "universe"). Thus, it offers direct protection, care, and defense not so much to individuals or even to the group, but to the idea itself. Indeed, this concept of crime extends the scope of judicial decision making to factors and aspects outside the objective and formalistic guilty conduct of the individual. But the main objectives of this extension of scope are limited to the involvement of the safeguarded ideology and, on the basis of its doctrines, to the consideration of some modern tariff for criminals and their victims.

The norms of responsibility and the evaluation of the criminal-victim relationships have to yield to the supremacy of the governing political idea. "The Soviet distinction," writes Harold J. Berman, "between theft of personal and theft of state property is probably an essential feature of a socialist system."[65] In general, he continues, "not merely the act but the 'whole man' is tried; at the same time, his crime is considered in the context of the 'whole community.' "[66] In systems where social control is based on the ideology-directed social defense against social danger, the interpretation of responsibility is necessarily subjective. The doer-sufferer relationship is viewed from the angle of this set of ruling doctrines; the responsibility is distributed and the degree of responsibility is evaluated in accordance with the ideological-social value of the victims or other crime targets.

The suprauniversalistic concept of crime is even more emphatically expressed in systems where responsibility is exclusively determined by judgment of the offender's personality; the victim's position depends entirely upon this judgment, regardless of his objective suffering and relationship with the criminal. The German *Täterstrafrecht* (criminal law as it involves the criminal), as it was seen in the past, tended to disregard the crime completely and to establish the degree of responsibility solely in accordance with the personality of the criminal. This somewhat distorted revival of Lombroso's extreme and unacceptable atavism theory intended that the judgment of human conduct be dictated entirely by the supreme ideology and that the offender be separated from his objective relation to his victim. In accordance with such a proposition, the victim's injury or harm, as well as his contribution to the crime, would lose importance.

The suprauniversalistic approach attempted to find the "normative type" of criminal, concerning whom the penal consequences of the criminal responsibility would be decided by the deviation of his personality (and not his actions) from the norm. The question of whether a murderer-type, a thief-type, a forger-type, a rapist-type, or any other type of criminal does or does not exist is a constantly recurring one in criminology. In the suprauniversalistic conception, however, recidivism, childhood experiences, pathological state of mind, or some other well-known causative factor does not start one thinking; only the criminal's phenomenally recognized total personality does so. While typological classifications are generally designed for preventive or reformative purposes, this normative typology was designed to assign the right responsibility to the right person. According to the suprauniversalistic typology, for example, capital punishment should not necessarily be inflicted on a person who actually committed a murder, but on any individual who, in view of his total personality, should be regarded as a murderer, regardless of whether he committed a homicide or not. Naturally, this raises the question of accurately defining the victim.

The *Volksanschauung* (public view) cannot be satisfied with a simple "symptom" (this is the criminal offense), because the criminal is not always what one particular crime makes him appear to be. From this viewpoint, a single symptom (the crime alone) should not determine the direction, scope, and weight of responsibility; nor should the responsibility be determined by any element of the criminal-victim relationship. Eric Wolf claimed that "political liberalism and religious naturalism" are over, and therefore "ethically indifferent positivistic individualism" should be replaced by "phenomenological personalism."[67] Wolf as well as Georg Dahm, the pioneers of this normative typology, emphasized a totalitarian idea of crime and suggested that *Volksanschauung* operate first of all in cases of "disobedience and resistance" against the "national socialistic state."[68] In this instance the offender's stand against the state is judged, rather than the criminal-victim relationship.

Since totalitarian ideologies emphasize the importance of the broadest social aspects, social cohesion, and extensive social responsibility, their penal policy may be mistaken for a universalistic understanding of the crime problem. However, they are suprauniversalistic in nature. There are profound differences in the historical development as well as in the societal context and goal of the two orientations. While the universalistic orientation aims at a harmony among conflicting responsibilities and tries to see them in their functional operation, the suprauniversalistic views are highly ideology-directed and for the sake of the ruling idea tend to disregard the victim's positive or negative contribution to crime. Not the personal drama of the criminal and his victim, but the drama of the offender and the ideology is of paramount and guiding importance. The suprauniversalistic concept of crime has substituted for the personal victim the idea of a victimized ideology. Here again, as in the distant past, the human victim loses his functional role when the crime is judged, and he is called to the stage only if he personally represents the doctrines or if the attack against this ideology can be proved only through the fact of his victimization.

Nonmaterial crimes, like treason, libel, or others, are known in criminal law; but the suprauniversalistic orientation gave rise to the idea of the metaphysical victim.

The Functional Responsibility of the Criminal and His Victim

The universalistic interpretation of crime and, along with it, the revival of the victim's importance are in their early stages. They face a struggle to achieve further development and recognition. This is one reason why the victim is still kept from playing an important role in criminal procedure. Another reason may be a misinterpretation of "universalism" in the judgment of crime: the victim is not included in the definition of the "universe" and is still regarded as if he were only a separate individual and not a part of the whole. Continued neglect of the victim may also be due to a sort of correctional ossification; the hardening of traditional patterns of deterrence and retribution leaves little room for him to function in the penal system. Deterrence and retribution have had a consistent and uninterrupted success for hundreds of years as the most essential and dominant of all penal elements. They are always made to fit the individualistically interpreted injury to the victim, regardless of whether they are called punishment, treatment, rehabilitation, correction, or something else. The penal systems of our world are formally open to an understanding of the "universe" and to a consideration of the assumption about treatment. In fact, however, they are still thoroughly riddled with individualistic security distinctions. They appear to remain retributive in their basic character. They do not operate in conjunction with all social forces that are involved. And they offer only a ritual restoration of law and order. Retribution is still practiced by making the criminal aware of the wrong he has done against the state and, as a socialized vengeance, by inflicting upon him various physical and psychic disadvantages for having wronged the victim. This may protect a number of future victims but does not defend those who have already been victimized. Nor does it utilize the criminal-victim relationship in the understanding and judgment of crime and in correctional methods.

Although it is doing so gradually and slowly, the universalistic approach has nevertheless started to include the victim in the attempt to understand crime. It has started to view the structural characteristics of crime and the variable quantity and quality of the criminal's responsibility in relation to that of his victim. The universalistic orientation tends to avoid isolating, on the one hand, the criminal and his crime and punishment and, on the other hand, the victim and his harm, injury, or other hurt. The particular activity of each and their relationship to each other and to the social values determine their correlate functional responsibilities. This changed attitude toward the victim has moved the revival of his importance in two directions: toward compensation or restitution for the wrong done to him by his criminal and toward his admission to the universe of factors without which crime cannot be understood. Rethinking the concept of responsibility and including the victim's role in the understanding of the crime problem would socially metabolize the increasing tendency to turn from the act-oriented criminal law to an actor-oriented judgment of crime.

NOTES

1. Stephen Schafer, *Restitution to Victims of Crime* (London and Chicago, 1960), pp. 3–12, 2nd ed. (Montclair, N.J., 1970).

2. Marvin E. Wolfgang, "Victim Compensation in Crimes of Personal Violence" (paper presented to the meetings on the American Society of Criminology, Montreal, 1964), p. 2.

3. E. Adamson Hoebel, *The Law of Primitive Man* (Cambridge, Mass., 1954), pp. 53, 116, 120, 311; see also Wolfgang, *op.cit.*

4. Ferenc Mádl, *A deliktuális felelősség* (Budapest, 1964), p. 52.

5. Rudolf Ihering, *Geist des römischen Rechts* (Leipzig, 1873), Vol. I, p. 118.

6. Wolfgang, "Victim Compensation in Crimes of Personal Violence," p. 3.

7. K. Jordan, "Adhäsionsprozess," in Weiske, ed., *Rechtslexikon für Juristen aller tentschen Staaten enthaltend die gesamte Rechtswissenschaft* (Berlin, 1839), Vol. I, pp. 122–23.

8. Richard R. Cherry, *Lectures on the Growth of Criminal Law in Ancient Communities* (London, 1890), p. 10.

9. William Tallack, *Reparation to the Injured, and the Rights of the Victim of Crime to Compensation* (London, 1900), pp. 6–7.

10. Exodus, 21:18, 19.

11. Cherry, *Lectures,* p. 11.

12. Minocher J. Sethna, *Society and the Criminal* (Bombay, 1952), p. 218; and *Jurisprudence* (2nd ed., Girgaon-Bombay, 1959), p. 340.

13. Margery Fry, *Arms of the Law* (London, 1951), p. 124.

14. John L. Gillin, *Criminology and Penology* (New York, 1945), p. 337.

15. Herman Ortloff, *Der Adhäsionsprozess* (Leipzig, 1864), p. 6; Karl Binding,

Gundriss des Deutschen Strafprozessrecht (Berlin, 1904), p. 115; Adolf Schönke, *Beitrage zur Lehre vom Adhäsionprozess* (Berlin and Leipzig, 1953), p. 5.

16. In German laws the word "punishment" (*Strafe*) first appeared in sources of the fourteenth century; Herman Conrad, *Deutsche Rechtsgeschichte* (Karlsruhe, 1954), Vol. I, p. 69.

17. Evelyn Ruggles Brise, *Report to the Secretary of State for the Home Department on the Proceedings of the Fifth and Sixth International Penitentiary Congresses* (London, 1901), pp. 50–51.

18. Cherry, *Lectures*, p. 10.

19. Bernhard Rehfeldt, *Die Wurzeln des Rechtes* (Berlin, 1951), p. 11.

20. Harry Elmer Barnes and Negley K. Teeters, *New Horizons in Criminology* (New York, 1944), pp. 400–401.

21. E.B. Tyler, *Anthropology* (New York, 1889), p. 415; quoted by Gillin, *Criminology and Penology*, p. 338.

22. Hans von Hentig, *Punishment, Its Origin, Purpose and Psychology* (London, 1937), p. 215.

23. Tacitus, *Germania*, Chapter 21; quoted by Gillin, *Criminology and Penology*, p. 338.

24. Barnes and Teeters, *New Horizons*, p. 401.

25. Irving E. Cohen, "The Integration of Restitution in the Probation Services," *Journal of Criminal Law and Criminology*, 34 (January-February 1944), 315.

26. Ephraim Emerton, *Introduction to the History of the Middle Ages* (Boston, 1888), pp. 87–90; Barnes and Teeters, *New Horizons*, p. 401; Edwin H. Sutherland, *Principles of Criminology* (4th ed., Chicago, 1947), p. 345.

27. Gillin, *Criminology and Penology*, p. 338; see also Wolfgang, "Victim Compensation."

28. Frederick Pollock and Frederic William Maitland, *The History of English Law* (2nd ed., Cambridge, 1898), Vol. II, p. 451.

29. Barnes and Teeters, *New Horizons*, p. 401.

30. Clarence R. Jeffery, "The Development of Crime in Early English Society," *Journal of Criminal Law, Criminology and Police Science*, 47 (March-April 1957), 645–66; quoted by Wolfgang, "Victim Compensation," p. 6.

31. Pollock and Maitland, "History of English Law," p. 451; Rustem Vámbéry, *Büntetőjog* (Budapest, 1913), Vol. I, p. 68; Pál Angyal, *A magyar büntetőjog tankönyve* (Budapest, 1920), Vol. I, p. 18.

32. F. Beyerle, *Gesetze der Longobarden* (Weimar, 1947), p. 62.

33. Heinrich Oppenheimer, *The Rationale of Punishment* (London, 1913), pp. 162–63.

34. Karl Binding, *Die Entstehung der öffentlichen Strafe in germanisch-deutschem Recht* (Leipzig, 1908), p. 32; Angyal, *A magyar büntetőjog tankönyve*, Vol. I, p. 18.

35. Pollock and Maitland, "History of English Law," p. 451.

36. Fry, *Arms of the Law*, p. 32.

37. A.B. Schmidt, *Die Grundsätze über den Schadenersatz in den Volksrechten* (Leipzig, 1885), pp. 9–16; Binding, *Die Entstehung,* p. 34.

38. Pollock and Maitland, "History of English Law," pp. 458–59; L.J. Hobhouse, G.C. Wheeler, and N. Ginsberg, *The Material Culture and Social Institutions of the Simpler Peoples* (London, 1915), pp. 86–119.

39. Wolfgang Starke, *Die Entschädigung des Verletzten nach deutschen Recht unter besonderer Berücksichtigung der Wiedergutmachung nach geltendem Strafrecht* (Freiburg, 1959), p. 1.

40. J. Makarewicz, *Einführung in die Philosophie des Strafrechts auf entwicklungsgeschichtlicher Grundlage* (Stuttgart, 1906), p. 269; Rehfeldt, *Die Wurzeln des Rechtes,* p. 17; Conrad, *Deutsche Rechtsgeschichte,* pp. 220–21.

41. D.M. MacDowell, *Athenian Homicide Law in the Age of the Orators* (Manchester, 1963), pp. 1–9.

42. Tallack, *Reparation to the Injured,* pp. 11–12.

43. H.F. Pfenninger, quoted by Thomas Würtenberger, "Über Rechte und Pflichten des Verletzten im deutschem Adhäsionsprozess," *Festschrift,* Prof. Dr. H.F. Pfenninger, Strafprozess und Rechtsstaat (Zürich, 1956), p. 193.

44. M. Voigt, *Die XII Tafeln* (Leipzig, 1883), pp. 538–39.

45. Josef Kohler and E. Ziehbart, *Das Stadtrecht von Gortyn und seine Beziehungen zum gemeingriechischen Rechte* (Göttingen, 1912), pp. 76–80. See also Ferenc Madl, *A deliktuális felelosseg,* pp. 112–13.

46. T. Mommsen, *Römisches Strafrecht* (Leipzig, 1899), pp. 3–6.

47. Karl Binding, *Normen* (3rd ed., Berlin, 1916), Vol. I, pp. 433–79; Sutherland, *Principles of Criminology,* p. 14.

48. Schönke, *Beitrage zur Lehre,* p. 11; Hans Heinrich Jescheck, "Die Entschädigung der Verletzten nach deutschem Strafrecht," *Juristenzeitung* (October 17, 1958), p. 592.

49. Schönke, *Beitrage zur Lehre,* pp. 28–42; Jescheck, "Die Entschädigung," p. 592.

50. Edwin H. Sutherland and Donald R. Cressey, *Principles of Criminology* (7th ed., Philadelphia, 1966), p. 331.

51. Tallack, *Reparation to the Injured,* p. 3.

52. Samuel J. Barrows, *The Sixth International Congress, Report of its Proceedings and Conclusions* (Washington, 1903), p. 23.

53. Raffaele Garofalo, *Criminology* (Boston, 1914), pp. 434–35.

54. See some of the details in Schafer, *Restitution to Victims of Crime,* pp. 9–11.

55. Hentig, *Punishment,* pp. 216–17.

56. Carlo Waekerling, *Die Sorge für den Verletzten in Strafrecht* (Zürich, 1946), p. 15.

57. See Schafer, *Restitution to Victims of Crime,* pp. 18–100.

58. Sutherland and Cressey, *Principles of Criminology,* p. 576.

59. Ferdinand Tönnies, *Fundamental Concepts of Sociology: Gemeinschaft and Gesellschaft,* trans. Charles F. Loomis (New York, 1940).

60. Wolfgang, "Victim Compensation in Crimes of Personal Violence," p. 2.

61. Ibid., pp. 10–11.

62. Robert A. Nisbet, "The Study of Social Problems," in Robert K. Merton and Robert A. Nisbet, *Contemporary Social Problems* (2nd ed., New York, 1966), p. 22.

63. Tallack, *Reparation to the Injured,* pp. 10–11.

64. Stephen Schafer, "Correctional Rejuvenation of Restitution to Victims of Crime" (paper presented to the meetings of the American Society of Criminology, Montreal, 1964), pp. 7–11.

65. Harold J. Berman, *Justice in the U.S.S.R.* (rev. ed., New York, 1963), p. 163.

66. Ibid., p. 257.

67. Eric Wolf, *Vom Wesen des Täters* (Berlin, 1932).

68. Georg Dahm, "Die Erneuerung der Ehrenstrafrecht," *Deutsche Juristenzeitung* (1934).

2

Criminal-Victim Relationship
as a Crime Factor

The Beginning of Victimology

The Founders of Victimology

The revival of the victim's importance tends to involve, among other things, the criminal-victim relationship as a partial answer to the crime problem. While compensation or restitution deals with the victim's role and the possibility of correction of the criminal in the postcrime situation, the criminal-victim relationship may point to the genesis of a crime and to a better understanding of its development and formation. "That the victim is taken as one of the determinants, and that a nefarious symbiosis is often established between doer and sufferer, may seem paradoxical. The material gathered, however, indicates such a relation." If this relation can be confirmed, and if the criminal-victim interactions and personal relationships can be observed in the "functional interplay of causative elements," crime can be seen and understood in a broader perspective. Revival of the victim's role in criminal proceedings not only means participation in his own behalf, but may also indicate his share in criminal responsibility.

Hans von Hentig might not have been the first to call attention to criminal-victim relationships, but, in the postwar period, his pathfinding study made the most challenging impact on the understanding of crime in terms of doer-sufferer interactions and invited a number of contributions to this aspect of lawbreaking. He seemed to be impressed by Franz Werfel's well-known novel, *The Murdered One is Guilty (Der Ermordete ist schuld)*, and suggested that the victim himself is one of the many causes of a crime. Hentig hypothesized that, in a sense, the victim shapes and molds the criminal and his crime and that the relationship between perpetrator and victim may be much more intricate than our criminal law, with its rough and mechanical definitions and distinctions, would suggest.

Hentig suggested that a reciprocality exists between criminal and victim. He often found a mutual connection between "killer and killed, duper and dupe." "The mechanical outcome," writes Hentig, "may be profit to one party, harm to another, yet the psychological interaction, carefully observed, will not submit to this kindergarten label." A mutuality of some sort raises the question of the dependability of external criteria, because, Hentig observes, the sociological and psychological aspects of the situation may be such as to suggest that the two distinct categories of criminal and victim in fact merge; it may be the case that the criminal is victimized.

Hentig backed his hypotheses with statistical data, documented fragments of experiences, and unstructured observations; but he did not support them by empirical research. However, his highly logical and vigorous speculations aided the revival of the victim's importance in the understanding of criminal problems. The concept of the "activating sufferer," who plays a part in "the various degrees and levels of stimulation or response" and who "is scarcely taken into consideration in our legal distinctions," is not original with Hentig, but his pioneering role and its great impact cannot be denied.[1]

Beniamin Mendelsohn claims that he originated the idea.[2] He refers to his article, published a decade before Hentig's study, which, though not a study of the victim, led him to his "gradual evolution towards the conception of Victimology."[3] Mendelsohn, as a practicing attorney, had his clients answer some 300 questions. His findings from this questionnaire led him to the conclusion that a "parallelity" appears between the "biopsychological" personality of the offender and that of the victim. After he published his first impressions,[4] he concentrated his investigation on the victim, first of all on rape victims and on the extent of their resistance.

In his basic study of criminal-victim relationships Mendelsohn proposes the term "victimology" in order to develop an independent field of study and perhaps a new discipline.[5] He views the totality of crime factors as a "criminogen-complex," in which one set of factors concerns the criminal and another the victim. He objects to "the co-existence of two parallel ways" and asks that they be separated. This divorce of the "penal-couple" (as he terms the criminal and his victim) would lead to "a new branch of science" —his victimology. Accordingly, he introduces a terminology for victimology. He proposes new terms such as "victimal" as the opposite of "criminal"; "victimity" as the opposite of "criminality"; "potential of victimal receptivity" as meaning individual unconscious aptitude for being victimized. He suggests the broadest possible acceptance and implementation of his idea. Thus he recommends the establishment of a central institute of victimology, victimological clinics, an international institute for victimological researches in the United Nations, an international society of victimology, and the publication of an international review of victimology. In Mendelsohn's view, victimology is not a branch of criminology but "a science parallel to it"; or, better, "the reverse of criminology."

Early Victim Typologies

Both Hentig and Mendelsohn attempted to set up victim typologies, but their classifications were speculative. Their work offers useful guidelines for research, but in the absence of systematic empirical observations it should be used with caution. In any case, the possibility of a spectacular variety of victim types is indicated, particularly by Hentig in his detailed list of such types. Mendelsohn distinguished between the guilt of the criminal and his victim; Hentig used a sociological classification.

In Mendelsohn's typology the "correlation of culpability (imputability) between the victim and the delinquent" is the focal point around which he gathered his victim types.[6] In fact, Mendelsohn's victims are classified only in accordance with the degree of their guilty contribution to the crime. They are grouped in the following categories:

1. The "completely innocent victim." Mendelsohn regards him as the "ideal" victim, and refers to children and to those who suffer a crime while they are unconscious.

2. The "victim with minor guilt" and the "victim due to his ignorance." Mentioned here as an example is the woman who "provokes" a miscarriage and as a result pays with her life.

3. The "victim as guilty as the offender" and the "voluntary victim." In explanation Mendelsohn lists the following subtypes:
    a. suicide "by throwing a coin," if punishable by law.
    b. suicide "by adhesion"
    c. euthanasia (to be killed by one's own wish because of an incurable and painful disease)
    d. suicide committed by a couple (for example, "desperate lovers," healthy husband and sick wife)

4. The "victim more guilty than the offender." There are two subtypes:
    a. the "provoker victim," who provokes someone to crime
    b. the "imprudent victim," who induces someone to commit a crime

5. The "most guilty victim" and the "victim who is guilty alone." This refers to the aggressive victim who is alone guilty of a crime (for example, the attacker who is killed by another in self-defense).

6. The "simulating victim" and the "imaginary victim." Mendelsohn refers here to those who mislead the administration of justice in order to obtain a sentence of punishment against an accused person. This type includes paranoids, hysterical persons, senile persons, and children.

Hentig's typology is more elaborate and uses psychological, social, and biological factors in the search for categories. He distinguishes born victims from society-made victims. He also sets up a victim typology in thirteen categories.[7]

1. The young
2. The female

3. The old
4. The mentally defective and other mentally deranged
5. Immigrants
6. Minorities
7. Dull normals
8. The depressed
9. The acquisitive
10. The wanton
11. The lonesome and the heartbroken
12. Tormentors
13. The blocked, exempted, and fighting

The young victim is an obvious type. Since the young are weak and inexperienced, they are likely to be victims of attacks. The young are easy victims not only because they are physically undeveloped, but because they are immature in moral personality and moral resistance. Though they are in the process of biological and cultural development, this cannot be fully complete in youth. However, the criminal's inner pressure to commit crime is normally a fully developed force against which the undeveloped resistance of the young is unable to compete on fair terms. Hentig suggested that since children do not own property, they are not usually victims of crimes for profit. However, a child may be murdered for profit if his life is insured. Kidnapping is an offense that usually involves the young. Further, children are frequently used by criminals to assist in committing crimes (mainly crimes against property).

In most countries laws are in force to protect children against involvement in moral turpitude, which indicates that they can be regarded even in this respect as victims. If the young person happens to be a girl, her victimization is well known with respect to sexual offenses. Leppmann, as cited by Hentig, pointed out that some young girls do not resist sexual assaults, and because of a mixture of curiosity, fear, physical inactivity, and intellectual challenge they do not try to escape from being victims.

The female is described by Hentig as a victim with "another form of weakness." Younger females sometimes become the victims of murder after suffering sexual assault; older women who are thought wealthy become victims of property crimes. The lesser physical strength of the female has greater significance than that of young people or children. While the criminal would find little point in committing a property crime against the propertyless young, this is not the case with regard to women. Women do have, or handle, things of financial value that may attract the criminal. Most offenders are men and therefore have the advantage of greater physical strength in crimes against women. Except in the case of rare homosexual offenses, women occupy a biologically determined victim status in sexual crimes.

The old are also likely to be victims in crimes against property. Hentig pointed out that "the elder generation holds most positions of accumulated wealth and wealth-giving power." At the same time old people are weaker physically and sometimes mentally. "In the combination of wealth and weakness lies the danger." Hentig suggests that old people are the ideal victims of predatory attacks. Their comparative weakness is behind proposed measures for their special defense, which would involve greater punishment for those who commit crimes against them.

The mentally defective and other mentally deranged persons are referred to by Hentig as a large class of potential and actual victims. It seems obvious that the insane, the alcoholic, the drug addict, the psychopath, and others suffering from any form of mental deficiency are handicapped in any struggle against crime. Hentig stated that of all males killed, 66.6 percent turned out to be alcoholics. He rarely found alcoholics among murder victims, but 70 percent of manslaughter victims were found to have been intoxicated. Often not only was the victim of manslaughter intoxicated, but the killer was also. Generally speaking, intoxicated persons are easy victims for any sort of crime, particularly property crimes. They are the targets of thieves, pickpockets, confidence men, gamblers, social criminals, and perhaps others. It has been demonstrated that crimes against persons in an intoxicated state are much greater than might be expected. As to the drug addict, Hentig refers to him as the "prototype of the doer-sufferer."

Immigrants are vulnerable because of the difficulties they experience while adjusting to a new culture. Hentig, who went through the immigration experience himself, points out that immigration is not simply a change to a new country or continent, but "it is a temporary reduction to an extreme degree of helplessness in vital human relations." Apart from linguistic and cultural difficulties, the immigrant often suffers from poverty, emotional disturbance, and rejection by certain groups in the new country. His competitive drive may evoke hostility. In these highly disturbing and conflict-producing situations, the inexperienced, poor, and credulous immigrant, who desperately clutches at every straw, is exposed to various swindles. It takes many painful years for him to adjust to a new technique of living; only then can he escape from being victimized. It is amazing that while people in general cannot fully perceive the difficulties of the immigrant, one category of the population—its criminals—understands the immigrant's disturbed situation and takes advantage of it.

The minorities' position is similar to the immigrants'. Lack of legal or real equality with the majority of the population increases the chances of victimization. Racial prejudice may increase their difficulties and can involve them in a victim situation. This may lead to violent criminal-victim relationships.

The dull normals, says Hentig, are born victims. He attributes the success of swindlers not to their brilliance but to the folly of their victims. The characteristic behavior of the dull normal is similar to that of immigrants and minorities; all three may be included in one category.

The depressed, as opposed to the previous "general" or sociological classes, are psychological victim types. Depression is an emotional attitude that is expressed by feelings of inadequacy and hopelessness, and that is accompanied by a general lowering of physical and mental activity. Sometimes it is pathological. Hentig suggests that the reciprocal operation of affinities between doer and sufferer can be measured in degrees of strength. The depressed person's attitude is apathetic and submissive, lacking fighting qualities. Resistance is reduced and he is open to victimization. Often the depressed person is weak not only in his mental resistance, but also physically, and this increases the possibility of his becoming a victim.

The acquisitive person is called "another excellent victim." Desire may not only motivate crime, but may also lead to victimization. Criminal syndicates, racketeers, gamblers, confidence men, and others exploit the victim's greed for gain. These victims can be found in almost every social strata: the poor man struggles for security, the middle-class man takes a chance in order to obtain luxuries, the rich man wants to double his money. It is well known that the latter category is the most vulnerable acquisitive victim.

The wanton is also one of Hentig's types, though he thinks of him as "obscured and dimmed by the rough generalization" of laws and social conventions.

The lonesome and the heartbroken are also seen as potential victims. Both are reminiscent of the acquisitive type, with the difference that it is not gain or profit but companionship and happiness that are desired. Hentig cites well-known mass murderers: Henri Désiré Landru, Fritz Haarmann, even Jack the Ripper; all took advantage of the loneliness and heartbroken feelings of their victims. Such credulous persons are not only victims of murder but are also, and more frequently, victims of theft, fraud, and other swindles.

The tormentor is a victim type who is found in family tragedies. Hentig gives the example of an alcoholic or psychotic father who tortured his family for a long time and who was finally killed by his son. Doubtless the latter was provoked by the father. This type of victim seems to be characterized by a lack of a normal prognostic sense. Consequently he strains a situation to such an extent that he becomes a victim of the tense atmosphere he himself creates.

The blocked, exempted, and fighting victims are Hentig's last category. By the blocked victim is meant "an individual who has been so enmeshed in a losing situation that defensive moves have become impossible or more injurious than the injury at criminal hands." Such is the case of a defaulting banker who has swindled in the hope of saving himself. Hentig refers here also to persons who are blackmailed; they are in a situation where the assistance of the police does not seem desirable. Hentig also refers to crimes of violence in which the victim fights back. In contrast to the "easy victim," this is the "difficult victim." Actually it would be better to exclude the fighting victim from the victim categories. Fighting back indicates resistance, thus this victim is less a victim type than the one whose resistance is overcome by the superior strength of the criminal.

Barnes and Teeters mentioned another victim type, the negligent or careless victim.[8] This type was later mentioned by others in connection with the problem of victim compensation. Barnes and Teeters referred to cases in which the victim's negligent or careless attitude toward his belongings makes it easy for the criminal to commit his crime. Inadequately secured doors, windows left open, unlocked cars, careless handling of furs and jewelry—these and other instances of negligence are an invitation to the criminal. They mention the theft of jewelry valued at $750,000 from the late Aga Khan. And they mention bank robberies in which the victims were responsible. An FBI survey reported that bank robbers were apprehended by guards in seven of the twenty-six institutions that employed guards; in two instances the guard was either at lunch or not on duty at the time of the robbery. The same survey revealed that too few employees take advantage of the protective devices that are available to them. In one instance, the teller pressed the alarm, but it did not work. It was learned afterward that the alarm system had not been checked for eighteen months.[9]

Another victim type, the *reporting or nonreporting* victim, is mentioned by Walter C. Reckless.[10] Here the victim is unwilling to report because he fears the social consequences of doing so. Reckless referred to blackmail and attempted suicide cases that remain invisible because of the nonreporting attitude of the victim. Henri Ellenberger, too, tried to classify victim types, but because his contribution is abstract, mention of it will be reserved for the section on speculative soundings about the victim.

This list of victim types could be extended but would not serve any purpose. Personal frustration has many forms, and negligence can be split into several types. Persons who are lonesome, heartbroken, or blocked may be reacting to certain situations and may not be types of victims. These situations may, however, serve as instructive examples of the important interactions and relations between the criminal and his victim. Thus, they can enlighten social situations, can call attention to victim risks, and may assist in determining responsibility; but they may fail to develop a general victim typology.

Continued Efforts to Develop Victim Typologies

Victim typologies attempt to classify the characteristics of victims, but actually they often typify social and psychological situations rather than the constant patterns of the personal makeup of victims. The "easy" victim and the "difficult" victim appear according to the balance of forces in a given criminal drama. The lonesome are prey to the criminal only when they are lonely. The heartbroken are easy victims only when they suffer a temporary disappointment. On this basis, hundreds of victim "types" could be listed, all according to the characteristics of a situation at any given moment.

However, there are indeed biological types of victims who, compared with temporary "situational" victims, seem to be continuously and excessively prone to becoming victims of crime. To be young, to be old, or to be mentally defective are not "situations" but biological qualities that indicate a more or less lasting vulnerability to crime. Apart from them, a typology of criminal-victim relationships —along with the patterns of social situations in which they appear —might hold more promise. It might increase the defense of those who cannot compensate for their weakness through their own efforts; it might elucidate and explain characteristics of victimizations; it might evaluate victim risks and accommodate crime control and social defense to them; it might develop a selective and universalistic rejuvenation of the responsibility concept. As the President's Commission on Law Enforcement and Administration of Justice put it, "If it could be determined with sufficient specificity that people or businesses with certain characteristics are more likely than others to be crime victims, . . . efforts to control and prevent crime would be more productive."[11]

Nevertheless, in spite of continued efforts, no good working typology of victims has developed as yet. The President's Commission on Law Enforcement and Administration of Justice appears to have leaned toward distinguishing between reporting and nonreporting victims. In doing so, the Commission excluded willful homicide, forcible rape, and a few other crimes which had too few reported cases to be statistically useful. Among those crimes not reported to law enforcement agencies, it listed robbery, 35 percent; aggravated assault, 35 percent; simple assault, 54 percent; burglary, 42 percent; larceny over $50, 40 percent; larceny under $50, 63 percent; auto theft, 11 percent; malicious mischief, 62 percent; consumer fraud, 90 percent; other frauds, 74 percent, sex offenses (except rape), 49 percent; and family crimes (such as desertion and nonsupport), 50 percent. These nonreporting victims were revealed in a national survey of households. According to their responses, they did not notify the police because they felt it was a private matter and did not want to harm the offender; they thought that the police could not be effective and would not want to be bothered; they did not want to take time; they were too confused and did not know how to report; or they were afraid of reprisal. It is admittedly not clear whether these responses are accurate assessments of the victim's inability to help the police or merely rationalizations of their failure to report,[12] but even if we assume that they are accurate, this distinction would not serve the development of a meaningful typology of victims because it does not always reflect to the criminal-victim *relationships,* and because it does not clearly explain those *victim characteristics* that would cause the victim's negative attitude and behavior; thus, it does not lead to the solution of the problem of responsibility.

A rather complex classification of victims has been offered by Ezzat Abdel Fattah, who designed five major classes with eleven subcategories, which still did not cover all possible victim types, nor did it indicate the possible distribution of responsibilities.[13] His main types are the following:

1. Nonparticipating Victims, who feel a denial or repulsion toward the crime and the criminal, and who do not participate in the origin of the crime committed against them;

2. Latent or Predisposed Victims, who (Fattah does not explain why) have certain character predespositions for being victimized by certain kinds of offenses;

3. Provocative Victims, who precipitate the crime, or even provoke it;

4. Participating Victims, who by their passivity or other similar attitude make their own victimization possible or easier; and

5. False Victims, who are not victims at all or who victimize themselves.

In their attempt to measure delinquency, Thorsten Sellin and Marvin E. Wolfgang have offered a kind of victim typology,[14] later somewhat refined by Wolfgang.[15] They have listed:

1. Primary Victimization, which refers to personalized or individual victims;

2. Secondary Victimization, where the victim is an impersonal target of the offender (e.g. railroads, department stores, churches, and the like);

3. Tertiary Victimization, which involves the public or the administration of the society as victim;

4. Mutual Victimization, which refers to victims who themselves are offenders in a given mutually consensual act (e.g., fornication or adultery); and

5. "No Victimization" where there is no immediately recognizable victim and which refers to acts of a minor nature or of negligible significance.

This typology appears to be aimed primarily at depicting crimes, and although it describes "situations," it does not reflect the criminal-victim relationships and responsibilities. Robert A. Silverman supported this classification with slight modifications, but even so, he, in his otherwise illuminating survey, failed to be concerned with the victim's specific characteristics.[16]

While their categorization seems to fall far below what is expected from a theory-backed victim typology, the influence of the character of the victim is more clearly spelled out by David Landy and Elliot Aronson, who distinguish between "attractive victims" and "unattractive victims" as they affect decision making in the administration of criminal law.[17] Even closer to what a victim typology should really mean is Gilbert Geis's approach: he has found the key issue in the factor of "victim responsiveness."[18] It is unfortunate, however, that he has restricted his thought to only white-collar crimes.

Hans Joachim Schneider has criticized all victim typologies for the absence of an empirical-factoranalytical basis.[19] However, he also appears to have failed in proposing classes which, as he claims, should embrace all possible types, should not overlap, and should be useful for practical as well as research purposes. Actually, he refers only to victim "aptness" and victim "inclination," pointing to victims of sex offenses, marriage swindles, group rapes, child abuses, social views, and the fear of crime.

Certainly no victim typology can be perfect, and in our present state of knowledge even the best would be easily vulnerable for a critique. Since human behavior cannot be labeled and classified in clearly individual categories, all typologies and classifications necessarily exhibit a more or less arbitrary and heuristic character. This is even more obvious if the proposed typology looks as if it were forced upon a general theory of crime or a specific theory of victimology (if any such theory exists at all), or if it is not backed by a general explanation of criminal-victim relationships and the characteristics of victims. The typology that floats in a vacuum is useless except as a point of departure for other typologists. As Stephen Schafer contended, this is why so many typologies seem to be only speculative guesswork or trivial impressions supported by more or less superficial experiences.[20]

A victim typology cannot be an independent venture in the understanding of the victim, his relationship with his criminal, or his responsibility in crime. Ideally, a typology should be derived from a single plausible hypothesis or a general theory of the concept of responsibility and criminal-victim relationships (explainability); it should be the observation of general distinguishing forms common to large numbers of crimes, criminals, victims, victim characteristics, and criminal-victim relationships, which can be used as a model to which they are referrable (reality); and it should be pragmatic, permitting its application to systematic grouping of types of victims and criminal-victim relationships so that the crime participants' (the victim's and his criminal's) responsibility can be assessed accordingly (instrumentality). A victim typology remains a meaningless speculation if it is not linked to a theoretical model and if it has no responsibility-guiding application; it should not be only a set of profiles, but it should also be a directive toward assessing responsibility. Modern trends lean toward the construction of types and empirical observations that may lead only to after-the-fact theoretical formulation. To early "victimologists," such as Hentig and Mendelsohn, the refinements of the statistical *tour de force* were not known, their theories came first, and their observations afterwards.

Although one might disagree with the idea that proposes to assess *the victim's responsibility,* this concept may operationally cover the pivotal issue in the criminal-victim relationship that, after all, is the critical problem of understanding and judging crime. Based on the idea of who is responsible for what and to what extent, the following victim typology may be here tentatively proposed:

1. *Unrelated Victims,* who have no relationship whatsoever with their criminal, except that the offender has committed a crime against them. All members of society are potential victims; all by definition are exposed to be victimized, regardless of whether they had any previous personal relationship with the lawbreaker.

Crime statistics indicate that a significant number of criminal offenses are purely one-sided decisions and acts of the criminal whose independent idea of violating the prohibitions of the criminal law has nothing to do with his relationship, if any, with the victim or with the victim's characteristics. The manager of the bank, for example, is not related to the bank robber, nor is the owner of the burglarized house; these and others are selected by the criminal as victims only randomly or by situational considerations of the planned crime, thus the criminal is supposed to carry the full responsibility.

2. *Provocative Victims,* who have done something against the offender who, consequently, has become roused or incited to victimize this doer-victim. In this case, the victim is the first doer. From a simple violation of a promise, through treatment with a scornful abuse, to having an affair with another's beloved, a great variety of the victim's doing against the criminal or his interest may prompt the offender to commit a crime that is directed to harm the victim. The responsibility in this case should be heavily shared.

3. *Precipitative Victims,* who have done nothing specifically against the criminal, but whose thoughtless behavior instigates, tempts, or allures the offender to commit a crime against the enticing victim. Walking alone at a dark deserted place, for example, may tempt the criminal to rob, or an overly revealing dress of a female may allure to rape. Naturally, a perfectly socialized person (if there is such a thing at all) is not supposed to be tempted or enticed to the extent of violating the rules of the criminal law, however strong or whatever the temptation or allurement might be. Yet, the characteristics of the criminal's personality are often bent by the characteristics of the victim's behavior toward committing the crime. In these cases the victim, since he ought to ponder the risk, cannot be seen as entirely blameless, and some responsibility should be carried by the victimized person.

4. *Biologically Weak Victims,* whose constitution or physical or mental characteristics develop in the offender the idea of crime against them. The child, the aged, the female, the disabled, the mentally sick or deranged, and others, though unrelated to the criminal, represent easy prey for the offender. Although in this respect the victim actually precipitates the crime, he could not and cannot do otherwise and thus should not carry any responsibility. If any part of the criminal's responsibility is to be shared,

it should be shared by the larger society or its governors, who did not provide the necessary protection for these partially or totally defenseless victims.

5. *Socially Weak Victims,* who are usually not regarded by the larger society as full-fledged members of the community. Immigrants, those affiliated with certain religions, ethnic minorities, and others who are in a socially weak position are often exploited by the criminal element. Socially weak victims are almost always blameless, and the responsibility ought to be heavily shared by both the criminal and the society that is responsible for the prejudice against them.

6. *Self-Victimizing Victims,* who victimize themselves and are thus their own criminals. Some sources tend to call their crimes "victimless" crimes, or "crimes without victims," but these terms, however spectacular, miss the point of the basic tenet that crimes, by definition, cannot exist without victims. Although most crimes involve two participants, the criminal and the victim, crimes can be immaterial acts (such as treason or espionage, for example) where only the criminal is visibly personalized and the victim may be the society as a whole or an idea. There are also crimes where the criminal and victim merge—but even in such cases, there are always victims. Drug addiction, alcoholism, homosexuality, and gambling are examples of those criminal offenses where the victim victimizes himself, or the interest of the society, and thus is a victimized criminal and plays a double role. The responsibility, therefore, need not be shared: it is to be carried by one person—the criminal-victim.

7. *Political Victims,* who suffer at the hands of their political opponents. Revolutionaries, who battle for their ideology, and lose, do not belong in this category: according to the concept of law they are to be regarded as criminals (who may become at a later time heroes). By definition, the ruling social-political power cannot victimize the violators of its prescriptions. In a certain sense, the victim precipitates the crime by striving for a political position. The ruling power, its supporters, or actually anybody, in the course of a campaign for a powerful position, may seek out, construe or magnify any mistake or offense for the purpose of *making* a criminal of the competitor who, in the ultimate analysis, should be regarded as a political victim. Although in the formalistic-legalistic sense he is to be qualified as a criminal, looking at him from a moral angle he should be classed as a victim having no sociological responsibility.

Speculative Soundings about the Victim's Role

Before empirical studies started to reveal the hidden realities in criminal-victim relationships, a number of speculative soundings were made, most of them based on abstract thought.

Iturbe agreed with Mendelsohn that a science of victimology should be created,[21] but Paul Cornil suggested that this is not a new departure and the term "victim," mainly as it appears in German and Dutch translation (the German, Dutch, and French words for victim are *Opfer, Schlachtoffer,* and *Victime*), seems to have some background as a religious reference to the sacrifice of a human being or of an animal.[22]

In an early article Hentig suggested that the reality of life "presents a scale of graduated interactivities between perpetrator and victim, which elude the formal boundaries, set up by our statutes and the artificial abstractions of legal science, that should be heeded by a prevention-minded social science."[23] In his view, there is a reciprocal action between perpetrator and victim. But, as mentioned before, chronologically Hentig was not the first in the field, nor was Mendelsohn. Prior to their studies, Jules Simon, among others, discussed the consent of the victim,[24] and Jean Hemard also approached criminal-victim relationships from the same angle.[25] Kahlil Gibran was talking about victim-precipitated crimes when he called attention to the fact that "the guilty is oftentimes the victim of the injured."[26] Ernst Roesner analyzed the statistical profile of murderer-victim relationships,[27] and Boven discussed the victim's role in sexual crimes.[28] Also before Hentig and Mendelsohn, provocation of homicide had been recognized as victim-precipitated by Rollin M. Perkins[29] and by Herbert Wechsler and Jerome Michael.[30]

In the 1950s, interest in the criminal-victim relationship increased. Rhoda J. Milliken asked that the postcrime sufferings of the victim be considered. Too often, she wrote, the victim suffers not only from the crime at the time it is committed but also from a series of events that "serve to scar deeply and sometimes damage irreparably the human being for whose protection the public clamors."[31] Tahon also focused attention on the problem of the victim's consent to a crime.[32] Henri Ellenberger discussed the broader psychological aspects of the victim's relationship with his criminal,[33] and suggested that, in the common sense understanding, criminal and victim, though interrelated, are as different as black and white. In his somewhat psychoanalytic approach he emphasizes the importance of considering the doer-sufferer aspect (*le criminel-victime concept*), the problem of the potential victim (*la victime latente*), and the special subject-object relation (*la relation spécifique criminal-victime*). He set up a list of psychological victim types, among others the murderer (criminal) of himself (victim): in other words, the person who commits suicide. Another of his types is the victim of "reflexoid" actions (discussed a half-century before by Hans Gross). Also, he called attention to the "deluded" or "fascinated" (from the German *Verblendung*) easy victims and, among others, to the "born" victim. In Ellenberger's view, special attention should be paid to "victimogen" factors and "future victims," since all individuals have the right to know the dangers to which their occupation, social class, or physical condition may expose them. He urges an investigation of the fundamental mechanisms of the criminal-victim relationship. His message is not so much for a better understanding of crime as for more crime prevention. As a result, Ellenberger became one of the pioneers in directing attention to the practical importance of victim risks. A similar line is followed by Werner.[34]

After many attempts at understanding criminal-victim relationships through psychological investigations, Erwin O. Smigel tried to explore a segment of this field from a more or less sociological viewpoint. He was concerned with theft from organizations as related to the size of the organization.[35] Socioeconomic status, sex, religiosity, and group membership served as his variables in testing attitudes toward stealing from victim organizations of different sizes. Ehrlich analyzed fraud—its method and its victim—primarily from the preventive point of view,[36] David Reifen discussed sexual crimes and their victims,[37] and Hans Schultz[38] and Souchet[39] made general remarks on victimology and on the criminological and legal relevance of criminal-victim relationships.

The Belgian publication *Revue de Droit Pénal et de Criminologie* devoted one issue to the problems of victimology and published several articles on understanding the criminal and his victim.[40] One of the contributors, Willy Calewaert, discussed victimology in relation to cases of fraud.[41] Aimée Racine discussed the specific behavior of child victims and suggested psychiatric examination or at

least social casework for young victims in certain instances.[42] De
Bray distinguished three phases of victim attitudes: those before,
during, and after the crime.[43] René Dellaert wrote about the dynamics of the criminal-victim relationship from a "cinéramique"
view. He observed the relationship from the angles of psycho-
technique, clinical psychology, social psychology, mental pathology,
preventive measures, and education.[44]

Noach tried to open up a new aspect of victimology, and focused
his attention on the interaction between the criminal and a collectivity as his victim.[45] It is unfortunate that his idea has not been
elaborated upon: the history of mankind, even of recent times, can
offer a great many illustrations. Leroy Schultz turned to an obvious
and well-known example of criminal-victim relationships when, in
commenting on interviews with the victims of sex offenders, he
suggested that a "portion of guilt" may be attributable to the victim.[46] Edwin D. Driver investigated the victim's role in crimes in
India and found that it is often possible for an affectionate or
friendly relationship to end in homicide.[47] Gibbens and Joyce Prince
analyzed the child victim of sex offenses. However, they seemed
interested primarily in the defense and protection of children, and
contributed little to the intricate relationship of the child and the
criminal.[48] Albert G. Hess, some two decades before, analyzed a
similar topic and offered data on the age, sex life, intelligence, and
social circumstances of the victimized children.[49]

Nagel meditates on the boundaries of "criminology" and suggests that if it were redefined as "criminology of relationships," victimology would not need to be considered as a separate discipline.
He calls attention to the fact that criminology is often misidentified
with criminal etiology; if it could be so identified, victimology
would be justified. However, Nagel proposes, the "counting, measuring, weighing, determining and comparing [of] victims"—and also
the "collecting of victimological determinants, factors, associations
and correlations"—will never achieve any great importance. Instead, he suggests "the removal of the conflict situation" between
criminal and victim should be the goal of criminal policy.[50] Reckless does not argue about the justification of "victimology," but he
does call attention to "victim proneness"; many victims are people
who tend to be victimized and are in a sense responsible for provoking criminal behavior. He goes on to say that forgetfulness or
absentmindedness may provoke crimes.[51] Abdel Fattah analyzed

"victimological" problems from a legalistic point of view. He questions the existence of harmony between the penal codes and scientific progress. His approach to the victim's responsibility refers largely to the legal position of the crime participants.[52]

Justification of "victimology" as an independent science or discipline may indeed be a questionable objective, but only adherents of the formalistic-individualistic interpretation of crime can oppose or devalue the victim's responsibility, the measuring, weighing, and analysis of the criminal-victim relationship, and the need for special attention to victim risks. The judgment of crime *is* formalistic; and necessarily so, unless one were to advocate anarchy; and it *is* individualistic, unless the human being were to be dissolved in a collective whole. But formalism and individualism cannot be goals in themselves, and should be understood from the viewpoint of all participants in crime and from that of the societal context of criminal justice. Criminal, victim, and their society—one comprehensive concept should embrace all.

Early Empirical Studies of the Victim

The studies that we have just reviewed concerning the problem of victimology or, better, the problem of the criminal-victim relationship indicate growing interest in aiding the revival of the victim's importance. However, all these studies, convincing and promising though they may seem, and though supported now and then by examples of crimes, criminals, and victims, suffer from the absence or insignificance of empirical evidence. In addition to studies of this kind, there are a few research studies of an essentially empirical nature, but even these seem to miss the central issue of the criminal-victim relationship. This issue is the functional responsibility for crime.

Among those empirical pioneers who attempted a closer understanding of the victim, one has to point out Marvin Wolfgang for his study of the patterns of criminal homicide,[53] in which "the relationship of the antagonists to one another"[54] has been systematically researched. It involved 588 homicide cases in Philadelphia, Pennsylvania, between 1948 and 1952 and included such aspects as race, sex, and age differences; methods and weapons used to inflict death; temporal and spatial patterns; alcohol and violence; previous police records; motives; personal relationships between victims and offenders; and victim-precipitation. The findings provoked a great deal of thought.

Evelyn Gibson and S. Klein, members of the English Home Office Research Unit, presented an analytic survey of murders known to the police in England and Wales from 1952 to 1960.[55] The important changes in English law that were made by the Homicide Act of 1957, which virtually redefined murder prompted a report on court proceedings and on victims and offenders in murder cases. The report was in the form of a purely statistical study based mainly on absolute figures, averages, and percentages.

Hunter Gillies made 66 psychiatric examinations of persons accused of murder between 1953 and 1964 in the Glasgow area in Scotland.[56] His examinations usually took place in a prison a few days or weeks after the arrest; but on seven occasions the interview was held at a police station a few hours after the arrest, and on three occasions it was held in a mental hospital. Gillies examined 59 male and 7 female offenders; no one else was present during the interviews.

Criminal-Victim Relationships in Violent Crime—A Study

Stephen Schafer examined criminal-victim relationships in violent crime in Florida.[57] The United Nations' International Group of Experts regarded the following crimes as major violent offenses:

1. Criminal homicide, including first and second degree murder;

2. Aggravated assault: the unlawful intentional disturbance of the physical well-being of a person, causing harm to the body or to health, if it results in a grievous, long-lasting, or permanent injury;

3. Theft with violence, including robbery and burglary: robbery is a completed theft that involves violence or threat, or that involves violence or threat when the offender is caught *flagrante delicto,* either while in the act of stealing or while attempting to escape; burglary is a completed theft that involves the use of force on things (not persons), or that involves unlawful entry, hiding on the premises, or the unlawful use of keys or other implements.[58]

However, these definitions were designed only to furnish a convenient basis for a planned uniform international crime reporting system. Thus, because they are rather arbitrary and deal in generalities, Schafer adapted them only as guides to the understanding of violent crime. In view of that, in this research the investigation of criminal-victim relationships in violent crimes was confined to Florida, and the definition of the three major offenses was accepted according to the provisions of Florida law; that is to say, the law of the place where the research was done, and as interpreted and applied by the courts. It was assumed and hoped that these crimes of violence would offer the best possible chance for observing the victim's positive or active participation in crime. This assumption was not borne out by the investigation, however. This was due partly to the almost complete absence of relevant data in official files and records, and partly to the reluctance of victims to reveal their roles in lawbreaking. One of the most important and instructive findings of the inquiry was the fact of official disregard of the victims' participation in crimes.

The research covered both the criminal cases and the characteristics of Florida's criminal inmate population from July 1, 1962 to June 30, 1963. This research was limited to those who had been incarcerated for any of the three major violent crimes.

Data was obtained through two questionnaires. One was used in all cases in which at least one answer could be obtained in addition to the answers concerning identification (name of inmate, sex, address, case number, and so forth). The other questionnaire (an extended form of the first) was applied to a random sample. This random sampling was administered according to the Random Numbers I and II of the Fisher's and Yates' Table XXXIII.[59] The combined questionnaires comprised 124 items, and possible answers were indicated by numerical symbols. According to the alphanumeric frequency count, out of the 124 items, 4 had to remain completely blank (because of the lack of answers or the obviously unreliable nature of answers), and 120 items were answered by all or part of those questioned.

The shorter questionnaire (the one used in all cases) was answered first from the records of the Florida Division of Corrections. After that the data was checked against, and completed by, the records of the penal or correctional institution in which the inmate was incarcerated. The longer questionnaire was put through the same process. In addition, however, information from the victim and a personal interview with the inmate served to complete the data as fully as possible. The first questionnaire was used in 721 cases; the second in 72 cases (10 percent of the former).

The research classified the inmates according to crimes committed as follows:

Criminal homicide	165
Aggravated assault	217
Theft with violence	306
More than one of these crimes	33
Total	721

Criminal-Victim Relationships

Victim Statistics

To say that the crime statistics cannot satisfy the demands of criminologists is a traditional cliché. Indeed, official crime statistics seem unable to cope with the difficulties of drawing an accurate picture of the amount of crime and the number of criminals; and victim statistics, if any, offer even less information. Ever since Moreau de Jonnés pointed out the difficulties of evaluating statistical data,[60] and Adolphe Quetelet urged the first session of the International Statistical Congress in Brussels in 1853 to develop "scientific" criminal statistics,[61] a long list of publications have recommended better techniques and more useful methods of describing the crime problem.[62] The despairing views of the Mixed Committee of the International Statistical Institute and the International Penal and Penitentiary Commission, released shortly before World War II, helped to keep alive the pessimistic school of thought in judging crime statistics.[63] A recent major effort has been made by the President's National Crime Commission, however, and hope must not be abandoned for a successful struggle against the "dark figures" and intelligent victim statistics.

At present, a number of factors distort the reliability of crime statistics. One is the emergence of certain "topical crimes." These are acts that are considered crimes only during the time of a specific temporary situation. Conduct is punished not because it is criminal; rather, application of the penalty creates the criminal. Changed economic conditions, war or revolution, political upheaval, and other transient conditions may prompt the ruling power structure of a society to change permitted conduct into prohibited conduct. This increases the number of both criminals and victims. Other factors also make it impossible to isolate accurately the number of these temporary offenders and temporary victims and may increase the statistical distortion.

Also, variations in the legal system can hamper observations: for example, changes in procedural provisions,[64] different methods in proceedings,[65] changes in administrative efficiency and policies,[66] or variations in court decisions. In the main, acts newly defined as crimes (new law) and variations in the definition of offenses are responsible for dislocations and distortions in crime statistics. This, too, may indicate that crime is made by law.

Variations in reporting also frustrate efforts to state the crime problem accurately. The social or economic power of "white collar criminals" may hinder or stop reporting; often the victim of certain crimes is reluctant to report because he fears discriminatory social consequences if it becomes known that he is a victim.

There are different types of crime statistics, which view crime from different angles. Police statistics, court statistics, correctional statistics, and other statistics may blur the statistical picture. Types of data, methods of collecting data, nomenclature—all differ in accordance with the purpose of each statistical work. "Uniformity is a constant problem of police statistics and this is true to a much greater extent for court and correctional figures."[67]

Crime statistics ought to be the "lawmaker's chart, compass, and lead,"[68] not only should they give facts, they should indicate an interpretation of these facts.[69] But today's researcher must use them despite all their shortcomings. It is due to necessity that "there seems to be a wide-spread disposition on the part of writers in the field of criminology, including many social scientists, to assume that published crime figures are sufficiently accurate to afford a basis for comparative studies as well as rather profound conclusions as to differences in crime trends among areas and states."[70] Crime statistics, to the extent that they present a numerical analysis of crime and criminals, are sources of error, and even less reliable knowledge is obtainable if they concern the victim. However, if critical analysis and controlling procedures are applied to official statistical tables, the merit of some statistics in a variety of crime problems can be readily recognized. Permissible generalization is one thing, and findings regarding a specific sample is another; it is unfortunate how often we tend to confuse them and to use the method of investigation of one for that of the other.

The Federal Bureau of Investigation suggests that "a crime rate for practical purposes should be considered as a victim risk rate"; and since the crime rate projects the incidence of crime to the given population (in other words, it is a statement of numerical proportioning), "crime rates do not represent the number of criminals but, more accurately, the number of victims."[71] In the very broadest sense this is true, yet this crude measure is hardly more than a general warning of victim-risks. It shows proportionately how much of the total population is exposed to the risk of victimization but does not demonstrate the wide variety of criminal-victim relationships that specifically indicate exposure to risk. Also, the difference between the clearance of offenses (called "police solution rate") and crimes actually committed may distort the figures: law enforcement agencies cannot be expected to work miracles, a perfect police force does not exist, and there is no place in the world where—at least in terms of surface figures—the number of victims would not surpass the number of criminals. In fact, the police solution rate seems to be decreasing, while the known number of victims has increased.[72] Furthermore, it is not only the unsolved crime that is a source of anxiety, but also the unsuspected crime.

The FBI *Uniform Crime Reports* provide certain characteristics of the victim with respect to murder. This analysis is related to the weapons used and to a percentage tabulation of murder victims by age, sex, and race. A recent edition presented the findings of a survey conducted in the metropolitan area of Washington, D.C., in which the age and place of residence of the victim and offender were compared. The *Uniform Crime Reports* and police employee data give a nationwide view of the number of police officers killed and the number assaulted, projected to geographic divisions and population groups.[73] However, no other direct information about the role of the victim is available, and the student of criminal-victim relationships must struggle along with a dearth of empirical data.

Lack of adequate victim-statistics is one reason for our lack of knowledge about the cost of crime. For decades there has been a deep concern about crime. The public is shocked by crime waves. People and politicians talk about a "war" against crime. Crime has become the favorite news topic after economics. There is a boom in public interest in crime. However, we just don't know how heavy a burden crime is upon American society. The total loss caused by crime is not known.

The *Uniform Crime Reports* for 1965 partially estimates the value of property stolen at $629,700,000; 52 percent of it ($324,-500,000) is said to be recovered.[74] Stolen automobiles head the list with the highest loss ($332,900,000); but stolen currency, notes, jewelry including precious stones, furs, and clothing also considerably raise the cost of crime. The late J. Edgar Hoover, Director of the FBI, some time ago estimated the total at $22 billion, an amount much greater than annual donations to churches, and averaging about $500 for each American family.[75] In 1931 the Wickersham Commission (more properly named the National Commission on Law Observance and Enforcement) made a careful study of the subject, and estimated that the administration of justice, institutional costs, private insurance and protection, law enforcement, and related items alone cost a billion dollars. This amount of course, is apart from the amount lost to crime itself, and apart from the thousands of nonmaterial effects of crime, mainly crimes against the person (homicide, rape, kidnapping, assault, and so on).[76]

Donald R. Cressey is not alone in suggesting that these estimates are completely worthless: "In the first place, they are principally guesses; and in the second place, they are based on unwarranted assumptions."[77] Barnes and Teeters suggest that crime is known to be "fantastically" expensive, but "it is difficult to estimate even its approximate cost."[78] Gerhard Mueller rightly thinks that on the dollar cost of crime "we are totally in the dark."[79]

Sex Differences

The difference in crime rates between males and females has been obvious ever since the volume of crime has been observed from a statistical viewpoint. Everywhere throughout history men have committed more crimes than women.

The sex difference in crime rates is not well understood, and there have been different explanations. Lombroso studied the problem and proposed as an explanation that prostitution was a substitute for crime. According to his hypothesis, if the full scope of prostitution were known and if it were to be regarded as a crime, the crimes of the two sexes would be roughly equal in frequency.[80] Napoleon Colajanni proposed that males and females would commit a similar amount of crime if they were equally exposed to societal factors.[81] Otto Pollak also contended that the tendency toward crime in males is not greater than that in females, but that the "masked" criminality of women hides their crimes from detection.[82] Schafer hinted at the presexual and postmenopausal states of females, and attempted to answer the question by referring to the different hormonal balances.[83]

There is much disagreement about the quantitative difference between the criminality of the two sexes; at best the degree of this difference can be explained by cultural and social forces. The *Uniform Crime Reports* show that in the United States, for all criminal offenses, men are arrested eight or nine times more often than women. However, in the case of violent crimes (homicide, aggravated assault, theft with violence) female offenses are even less frequent; males are arrested some fifteen or sixteen times more often than females. Schafer found slightly more female aggravated assaults than female thefts with violence.[84] Wolfgang, who combined sex and race factors, came to the conclusion that "the difference in the frequency of criminal homicide is significantly greater between the races within each sex than the difference between the sexes within each race."[85]

The statistics for victims are not markedly different from those for criminals: here, too, there is a lower proportion of females. The President's National Crime Commission found that the rates of victimization shown for certain indexed offenses against men are almost three times as great as those for women.[86] However, the proportions appear much closer in violent crimes. In homicide, assault, burglary, and robbery cases males are victims of crime only about four times more often than females, a proportion significantly different from that when the two sexes are compared as offenders. To put it another way, females are more often the victims of violent crimes than of other kinds of crime.

The proportion of male to female homicide victims seems to be atypical; comparisons tend to confuse any attempt at a universal social diagnosis. In Schafer's findings in Florida, 43 percent of the homicide victims were females, a ratio of almost one to one.[87] Wolfgang found in Philadelphia, among white homicide victims, that

27 percent were females, a ratio of approximately three males to one female.[88] In England and Wales, however, female murder victims consistently outnumber male victims; the proportion is about three to two.[89] Veli Verkko claimed that as a general rule the proportion of female homicide victims is small in countries where the frequency of crimes against life is relatively high[90]; but this does not seem to apply to England and Wales, where criminal statistics show a rather high rate of murder. In any case, the legal definition of murder and other forms of homicide is different in different states and countries; in the absence of reliable comparative tools, no international analysis can be made without error.

Hentig attributed the high proportion of female victims to the fact that the female is relatively weaker; in other words, the female can be overcome by the superior physical force of the male.[91] However, this assertion would be valid only if it were true that all or most violent cases of crime involve male doers and female sufferers; or if it could be hypothesized that in these male-against-female dramas the female's conduct precipitated or provoked more violence than did a male's conduct in the clash. Schafer's findings do not support Hentig's speculations, because in Florida male criminals attacked males over three times as often as females, and female criminals attacked females seven times more often than males.[92] This would indicate that males not only constitute the great majority of criminals, but also are exposed to a higher victim-risk in violent crimes than females.

Crimes committed by the male outnumber those committed by the female—not only in general and in crimes of violence—but also in all age groups. Male criminality is slightly higher between the ages of 41 and 50; female criminality is slightly higher (but still considerably less than male criminality) among women who are 51 or older. Age groups of victims correspond roughly with those of criminals; this becomes obvious if it is assumed that crimes of violence most often occur in personal situations in which difference in age of those concerned is not strikingly great. Nevertheless, among males, those most frequently victimized are those who are under 21 or over 51 years of age. But in the oldest age group—61 and over—clearly the largest group of sufferers are females. The longstanding speculation about the old woman as a victim type is supported by empirical data.[93] Also, the longer life span of females might be one explanation for the heavier proportion of victimized old women; since women live longer, there is a greater chance that they will be victimized. Old women may be exposed to higher victim-risks for other reasons as well. Physically they are weak; they may be defenseless if they have suffered social rejection; often they keep their money and their valuables in their homes; they may feel insecure and lonely; they may be egotistic and thus irritate the younger generation. Other factors, including regression within the personality structure and the particular relationship of the senescent individual to the social environment may also expose them to higher victim-risks.

Interpersonal Relationships

Since motives cannot direct action in a vacuum, the interpersonal relationship of victim and criminal is of prime importance.[94] Mobilization of energy toward criminal activity and the level of emotions that directs behavior are often influenced by the particular relationship of the doer and his sufferer. The marital status of the offender and/or the victim—or the fact that one person is the spouse, child, parent, or other relative; or a friend or an acquaintance of the other person, or a stranger (third person) to him—may contain the seeds of a crime.

It has been shown that in Florida the greatest number of violent criminals was among married persons of both sexes; the smallest number was among widowed and divorced persons. This may cast some doubt on the validity of the general belief that marriage must take credit for having a strong restraining influence on crime. This assumption is based on the fact that in the overall prison population in America marital status shows up with definite significance in statistics: married men have the lowest rate of commitment, and divorced offenders the highest.

The significance of the family is supported, however, by other empirical data. In Florida more than half of the violent crimes were committed by persons who had no children in their household at the time of the crime. Moreover, criminality seems to decrease in almost direct proportion with the number of children in a family —from families with only one child to families of five or more. Children under 17 in a household had a strong correlation with a lower proportion of male criminals.

From the viewpoint of the victim, again married persons head the list for frequency. Married persons of both sexes are more often victims of violent crimes than persons in any other marital status. It has also been observed that legally divorced individuals are less often victims of violent crimes than those who are separated but not divorced. Among persons most often victimized (married individuals) and among those who are least exposed to victimization (divorced individuals) the relative number of females is higher than in any other category; among widowed persons, the two sexes are equal victim-risks. It might be conjectured that the responsibility that comes with marriage may expose a person to more conflicts than a single person is exposed to; and, if the matter is viewed from another angle, greater criminality may be expected from established married persons than from other individuals.

The marital and family status of the criminal participants—the sufferer and his doer—is more important if it concerns their interpersonal relationship. Almost all crime statistics evidence the dominance of the "stranger" (third person) victims, followed in frequency by those who are victimized by friends or acquaintances. Relatives, spouses, and children are attacked more than four times less often than those who are in other relationships with the criminal. However, the primary group contacts gain significance mostly in crimes against the person, and first of all in homicide cases. Wolfgang has shown that categories that involve close friends, family members, paramours, and homosexual partners constitute 65 percent of all criminal-victim relationships.[95] The President's Commission on Crime in the District of Columbia found that some 80 percent of the murder and aggravated assault victims and their offenders are acquainted or related.[96]

The frequency of close-contact victimizations is clearly detailed by Gibson and Klein. Their research in England shows that for over 40 percent of all women murder victims the suspect was the husband; for about 25 percent, the suspect was either a relative or a lover. However, they found the relationship of murder victim to criminal very different for men since, at least in England, very few women kill their husbands or lovers, and male victims are less often related in any way to the murderer.[97] In contrast to this, Wolfgang found that when a man was killed by a woman, "he was most likely to be killed by his wife," and when a woman was the homicide offender, "she was more likely than a man to kill her mate."[98] Schafer's investigation indicates that, relatively speaking, female criminals commit violent crimes against their spouses almost three times more often than do males, and nine times more often against their children. Also, violent crimes against friends and acquaintances are relatively more frequent on the part of females.[99] The President's National Crime Commission called attention to the finding that in 1965 killings within the family made up 31 percent of all murders, and over one-half of these involved spouse killing spouse and 16 percent parents killing children.[100]

Male criminals dominate the category of crimes against the stranger (third person). Despite the full emancipation of women, their area of conflicts seems to be smaller, and their less frequent contact with the outside world more or less confines their potential circle of crime to the family, relatives, and friends.

Age Differences

There is little disagreement in accepting age as one of the most decisive factors in crime. The division of offenders into juvenile delinquents and adult criminals goes back a century and has been introduced into most legal and penal systems of the world. The concept of youthful or young adult offenders, the consideration of the special aspects of the aging criminal, the classification of prisoners according to age groups—these and similar matters all claim our interest concerning age differences in crime. Age is one of the few crime factors that can be reflected in official statistics. Thus different age groups of offenders are open to a variety of investigations and analyses. Age groups of victims are not customarily classified, and no general statistical profile is available for them as it is for criminals.

In recent years the younger generation (20 years of age and under) has had the highest crime rate; the next highest rate is for adults between 30 and 39. The age group of 20 and under ranks high in thefts with violence (robbery and burglary); offenders in the age group of 21 to 29 rank high in criminal homicide and aggravated assault. Gibson and Klein's murder data for England, Schafer's research on violent crimes in Florida, and Wolfgang's study of homicide in Philadelphia reveal similar patterns.

The crime rate declines in the age group over 40. Younger offenders seem to be more interested in criminal profit; older offenders seem more likely to commit violent crimes for emotional reasons. Over the total life span, including those who are 61 and over, these patterns are quite pronounced. Thefts with violence decline in frequency with age. Criminal homicide increases with age.

As to age differences in the criminal-victim relationship, the indication is, as Wolfgang put it, "those who kill are younger than those who are killed."[101] Criminals seem to be five to ten years younger than their victims, at least in homicide cases. This difference does not change significantly in the case of female offenders, but they are of a higher average age. Pollak points out that women arrive at "the peak of their criminal activities" at a later age than men.[102] In other words, female crimes are delayed. Wolfgang's data for Philadelphia support this statement; they show that females in the age group of 25 to 29 commit homicides at about the same rate as males of 20 to 24. Similarly, in Gillies' sample, the mean age of the males is 28 and of the females 31.[103] However, females run a greater risk of becoming victims at a younger age than males. The President's National Crime Commission has shown that the victimization rate for women is highest in the 20 to 29-years age group, for men this falls in the 30 to 39-years age category.[104]

Schafer's Florida figures indicate that the closer the relationship of criminals to victims, the less frequent are violent crimes; also, the younger the offender the higher the frequency of crime. The figures also show that parents and children are least likely to be victimized. Only an insignificant proportion of violent crimes are committed against the spouse by persons under 21 years of age. This is explained by the fact that there are a relatively low number of married persons in this age group. Moreover, such persons are in an early and presumably happy stage of marriage. In the age group of 51 and over, the settled and presumably peaceful course of marriage is a factor in keeping down the frequency of violent crimes against the spouse.

However, as the data for Florida show, in the upper strata of the older age group (persons 61 or older), the spouse was the major target of violent crimes. In fact, this is the only age group in which almost half the violent crimes were committed against the spouse. Compatibility in marriage may not be true in the last lap of life; it is also possible that the feebleness and mental disorders that are sometimes found in old age can provoke one against his spouse. Generally speaking, in every age group the spouse is a victim of violent crime more often than the child, parent, or a relative. The latter are victimized primarily by those in the age group of 21 to 40.

Although strangers (third persons) are victims of crime more often than any other category in interpersonal relationships, this frequency is highest in the age group under 21, and decreases with the age of the criminal. The older the offender, the more his crime is likely to be committed against his family, relatives, and friends. The older the person, as Schafer's study in the City of Boston in 1974/1975 has indicated, the more likely is his victimization, particularly if the elderly is outside of his home. The primary offenders in such cases are members of younger age groups or juvenile delinquents engaged in crimes against property. This seems to be somewhat in contradiction to his previous findings in Florida, but it may be due to geographical differences since the elderly seem to be more protected in Florida.

In the United States, infants less than a year old account for over 1 percent of all murder victims; children under 14 account for some 16 percent.[105] In England this proportion is considerably higher; it is some 7 percent for infants less than one year old and over 26 percent for children under the age of 16. About three quarters of all victims among English children were murdered by a parent or older relative; girls between 5 and 16 ranked particularly high as murder victims in this category.[106]

Educational Background of the Partners in Crime

Education as a socializing institution may change attitudes and values, and is to a certain extent related to variations in crime rates. In 1940, among male prisoners over 25 years of age, 7.5 percent had not completed the first grade; less than 23 percent had completed the seventh or eighth grade; 5.6 percent had been graduated from high school; and less than 1 percent had had a college education.[107] In 1963 in Florida the author found that most violent criminals were in the group who had completed the fifth to eighth grades; next in number were the group who had completed the ninth to eleventh grades; the group who had completed the fourth or a lower grade were third in number. Out of 672 who had committed violent crimes he found only six with some college education and only four who were college graduates.[108] Women prisoners cannot be much different; as Ruth Shonle Cavan pointed out, in seven northern states their median educational level was slightly under the eighth grade.[109]

According to the Florida data, persons with a fifth- to eighth-grade education committed violent crimes more than four times more often than those who had been graduated from high school. The victims of these criminals did not differ significantly in their educational background. Most of them had completed the fifth to eighth grade, and the incidence of those with a college diploma was very low.

It looks as if criminals and their victims do not generally have specific differences in educational background; in other words, it looks as if they are of the same educational level. However, the relationship between criminal, victim, and education is not as simple as that. Persons of little education do not attack only people of little education, and college graduates do not confine their criminal offenses to victims with a degree. The effect of a formal education on criminality is not well understood. Lombroso was mistaken in pointing out that it is dangerous to educate a criminal mind.[110] Illiteracy does not contain the solution to the crime problem. It cannot be denied, however, that the relatively low level of education of offenders is a statistical truth.

Occupational Differences

Any standard textbook on criminology shows clearly that there is little disagreement about statistics that place the majority of offenders in the lower occupational brackets. To many of the authors this indicates that the offenders belong in the lower social classes. "Lower class" and "working class," though rather different in meaning, are used interchangeably in most studies. However, while *working class* refers to those who are engaged in physical labor (and might be the members of one or another social class), *lower class* has a number of aspects. Even if the amount of income were the main criterion, lower class and working class cannot be considered identical. "A position does not bring power and prestige because it draws a high income. Rather, it draws a high income because it is functionally important."[111] A considerable part of the working class draws a high income because it is functionally important; it therefore cannot be considered a part of the lower class.

Working class refers to occupation and focuses on a type of function; *lower class* is a position in the social stratification. Often they meet, but not necessarily. The lower class may represent only one subculture, even if this includes several sub-subcultures; but the working class might be represented in more than one subculture. The working class is functional not only as to the type of labor in which its members are engaged, and not only as a dispersed part of the society, but also in the understanding of the social structure. We might note here that distinguishing the working class from other classes is of major importance in Karl Marx's thought.

There is no agreement as to a method of measuring the differential placement of individuals in different sectors of the social structure; nor is there any agreement as to the criteria which could be used for ranking. In fact, there is no agreement even on the meaning of the term "social class" as a research tool.[112] At the same time, however, the lower class (whatever its composition and the criteria for it may be) and the working class are not indicators of either different or identical levels of the rather complicated and often confused formation of the social strata but of different conceptual groupings of the members of the society.

This is probably what led Gillies to state that murderers and most of their victims are predominantly of a low social class, although his findings do not indicate this clearly.[113] Wolfgang has little doubt that "at least 9 out of 10 offenders" in his homicide investigation were in the skilled, semiskilled, service, unskilled, and unemployed categories.[114] However, he did not identify occupational categories with class. Moreover, he questions the relationship between occupation and homicide. Occupation alone does not decide the commission of murder; many other factors have significant interplay. The same is true of the social classes; if it is a statistical fact that the majority of offenders belong to the lower class, this does not mean it is a social truth.

In the author's findings, most criminals and most victims were semiskilled or unskilled, and unemployed persons made up the second largest group both of criminals and victims.[115] However, there are differences in the rest of the groups. The third largest group of violent criminals consisted of craftsmen and foremen, but their victims came from the categories of managers, officials, and proprietors. Criminals in professional or technical occupations had a tendency to attack persons in a clerical or sales occupation; however, most victims in a professional or technical occupation were attacked by semiskilled, unskilled, and unemployed persons. Violent criminals in a clerical or sales occupation attacked mostly unemployed persons; however, most victims in a clerical or sales occupation were attacked by semiskilled, unskilled, and unemployed persons.

All this would indicate that the lawbreaking clash between criminal and victim does not occur primarily among persons in the same or similar occupational group. Violent crime has a rather mixed occupational background.

The proportion of male and female victims differs markedly in almost all occupational categories, with male victims predominating. However, there are approximately equal numbers of men and women among victims who are in clerical and sales occupations. In other words, in these occupational categories, at least according to the Florida findings, the risk of being victimized is almost equally high for males and for females.

The relatively low income of craftsmen, foremen, semiskilled, and unskilled persons, and the financial deprivation of unemployed persons should explain why so many of them are involved in crimes against property. Also, since emotional personal dramas develop so easily in rural areas, this may explain the higher rate of crimes against the person that are committed by farmers. However, the relatively high percentage of thefts with violence (robbery and burglary) committed by persons in a professional or technical occupation is not well understood.

The overwhelming majority of victims are strangers (third persons) to the offender. Probably the small size of communities in rural areas can explain why farmers are the ones who commit violent crimes most often against acquaintances. As mentioned before, their crimes are mainly against the person. In farm areas, almost all members of the community know each other; it can be assumed that this fact, plus the unavoidable tension that comes from living together in such an environment, contributes to the high rate of offenses against the person.

Spouses and children are victims in all occupational categories, but the Florida findings show that they are victimized mostly by unskilled and unemployed persons. A relatively high proportion of violent attacks against spouses was also found among farmers, managers, officials, and proprietors.[116]

Victim and Criminal Motives

Motive, as a factor that initiates and directs an action toward some goal or conditions one's conduct, is an essential element in any crime. Crime is always goal-oriented; without a motive it does not exist: even though the motive may operate on the unconscious level, and the offender may not be clearly aware of it. Even the criminal who is mentally ill has his motive for a crime, probably a sick motive that springs from his delusions. *Motive* is not the same as *intent*. The criminal intent, or *mens rea,* refers to the ability to deliberate: it may or may not exist, depending upon the mental state of the criminal. The motivation is the reason for the goal-directed action or conduct; thus it always exists. Intent and motive may be quite different in the same criminal case.

Motivation in human behavior may be based on biological or psychological needs, as well as on social forces. The variety of these activating factors permits the development of a variety of classifications of motives. Such classification of individual motives in different ways makes comparisons difficult, if not impossible. Often the motives of the offender are not defined and recorded at all; on other occasions they are recorded according to arbitrarily detailed reasons for the crime. Altercation, domestic quarrel, jealousy, revenge, financial gain, sexual drive, avoiding arrest—these are only a few of the motives typically used in homicide studies. Financial need, profit-seeking, agitation, influence of alcohol or narcotics, mental disturbance—these are a list of motives of a more general nature.

Most studies indicate that criminal homicide and aggravated assault are usually committed under the pressure of strong emotion and that crimes against property usually involve the least emotion. There is such a wide range of detailed reasons for agitated emotions that, as Ralph Banay suggested, "the motives for killing can be assigned to an infinity of divisions."[117] Although heated arguments and disputes, domestic quarrels, and jealousy seem to be involved in a majority of homicide and aggravated assault cases, robbery is also an important motive for murder. Financial need and profit-seeking logically motivate crimes against property. Intoxication leads the criminal first of all to assault, less often to killing, and very rarely to crimes against property—except in the case of *actio libera in causa,* in which the offender premeditatedly becomes intoxicated in order to make it easier for himself to commit a crime.

Schafer observed that profit appears as a dominant motive in younger age groups, up to 30 years of age. Beyond this age its frequency declines. In the age groups over 30, agitated feelings or emotions occur with stronger and growing frequency, and profit motivation seems to fade. This indicates that aspiration for gain may incite a person to crime in the years before he reaches financial stability; after this time emotions are the primary factor in lawbreaking. The effect of alcohol is important mainly for those in the "drinking age," that is, from 21 to 50. This same age group accounts for the majority of mentally disordered offenders. Emotion almost exclusively motivates the aged criminal, probably because he is deprived of other motives for biological reasons.[118]

The motivation-sex correlation is not really different in the two sexes, although there are quantitative differences between the male and female criminality. In violent crimes, strong emotion is the dominant motive in both sexes. However, while the desire for profit (through robbery and burglary) ranks second as a motive in the case of male criminals, in the case of female offenders intoxication ranks second as a motivating factor. Data indicate that in Florida alcohol incites females to crime five times more often than the motive of financial need. In general, financial need appears as the least important motive among female offenders in violent crimes.

Males are the most numerous victims of violent crimes that are motivated by emotion or by the desire for profit. Elderly females also represent a relatively high proportion of victims in crimes for profit. If narcotic addiction or mental disturbance motivates the criminal, his victims are mostly females.[119]

Wolfgang found that in 44 percent of his homicide cases both the victim and the offender had been drinking.[120] Gillies suggests that the setting for murder is most often a drunken quarrel; even in his rather small group of cases "three drunken victims provoked their deaths at the hands of sober persons."[121] The President's Commission on Crime in the District of Columbia has shown that almost half of the victims and offenders had been drinking prior to the crime.[122] While in other cases we can speak about a conflict of motivations, here an "agreement" is present. If the conduct-directing motivation in a crime is doubled because it operates in both parties, the conflict between the criminal and his victim becomes a sort of agreement in which the offender also risks personal damage. Many motivation agreements end in victim-precipitated crimes.

The desire for gain leads to crimes against strangers (third persons), but very rarely, if ever, to crimes against a kinsman. However, emotional disturbance and alcohol proved to be the leading causes behind crimes against the spouse, relatives, and friends. Strong emotion appears as the only motive for crimes against one's own child; hardly any other motive for a violent crime can be imagined in this instance.

Most criminals who have committed crimes involving violence have been found to be in fair or good physical and mental health. The poorer the physical health of the offender, the higher the probability of his committing crimes against the person; crimes for profit (against property) have been committed mostly by criminals in good health. We do not know why this is so. Motives for crime are probably developed by psychological needs that are buried in the subconscious.

Victim Precipitated Crimes and Attitudes after the Crime

The fact that the victim may play the role of the major contributor to a crime has been known to the courts all over the world for a long time. The offender is usually sentenced accordingly. But Hans von Hentig is the man who brought this "duet frame of crime" to the attention of sociological analysts of the crime problem.[123] In Hentig's words, the crime-precipitating victim is an "activating sufferer," the shaper and molder of the criminal's lawbreaking behavior. Hentig meant that this type of victim provokes his own suffering. Wolfgang joins in this assumption by proposing that "except in cases in which the victim is an innocent bystander, the victim may be one of the major precipitating causes of his own demise."[124]

In a way, the victim is always the cause of a crime, even if the crime is motivated for abstract reasons such as intellectual integrity, freedom of religion, public health, the safety of a nation. All crimes necessarily have victims, and, necessarily, the existence of the victim or something material or immaterial that belongs to him makes for crime and may actually produce a criminal effect. However, as so often happens, the victim not only creates the possibility of a crime, but precipitates it. In other words, the victim may develop the direction of the offender's criminal conduct toward himself. Even if he is an innocent bystander, in certain cases his silent "bystanding" may make him not only a psychological accomplice, but at the same time the one who establishes the criminal motive and encourages the criminal action. He may motivate the criminal unconsciously. Or he may motivate him consciously, disregarding the risk he is taking. Or he may feel that his provocation is justified. Or he may want to be victimized. Van Krevelen pointed out that the child as a victim of an adult offense is an exception that only seems to be a truism. Sometimes the child arouses emotions in the adult that may lead the latter to criminal action—there is a type of child who is "the victim of his own personal appeal."[125]

In precipitating a crime the victim enters into it as an active participant, shares the actor's role, and becomes functionally responsible for it. When Wolfgang gives as examples of victim-precipitation those cases in which "the victim was the first to show and use a deadly weapon" or "to strike a blow in an altercation . . . in short, the first to commence the interplay of resort to physical violence,"[126] he refers to legally clear-cut precipitation. But the victim should be functionally responsible for a great many more types of motivating behavior. The goal of the criminal's conduct may be learned not only through open and direct provocation and not only in relation to the opportunity produced by the mere existence of the victim, but also in relation to the demands of the victim. The victim may intrude upon the criminal's behavioral system and influence or direct against himself the offender's problem-solving and decision-making processes. The victim's crime precipitation may range in intensity from making a person conscious of a criminal opportunity to simple passivity, a higher degree of irritation, incitement, instigation, or provocation.

Wolfgang found that 26 percent of his cases were victim-precipitated. In his homicide sample he revealed significantly high proportions of the following:

- Negro victims
- Negro offenders
- male victims
- female offenders
- stabbings
- male victims of female offenders

- male victims of spouse slayings
- alcohol consumed immediately prior to homicide
- alcohol in the victim
- victims with a criminal record
- victims with a previous record of arrest for assault.[127]

Schafer, in his sample, found that only 6 percent of the cases involved direct provocation by the victim; an additional 4 percent involved passivity on the part of the victim. However, there was a strong and significant correlation between the age of the offender and the victim's attitude. In his sample of violent offenses, in most crimes committed by persons in the age group of 21 to 30, the victim resisted attack. Passivity appeared mainly in cases in which the criminal attack was made by persons in the age group of 31 to 40. In general, the indication seemed to be that the older the criminal, the lower the resistance of the victim. The victim's resistance against offenders in the age group of 61 and older appeared to be nearly nil. Resistance may be a kind of provocation, it may increase the criminal effort; this may be especially true in sex crimes. The highest frequency of victim-provocation (clearly victim-precipitation) occurred in cases in which the offender was in the age group of 21 to 30.

As has been mentioned before, however, for the sake of a clearer insight, the popular term victim "precipitation" should be divided into the categories of victim "provocation" and victim "precipitation." Moreover, "precipitative" victim behavior should be further classified as to whether the victim carries any responsibility, and if so, how much. In the early empirical studies of criminal-victim relationships such distinctions were not proposed, except perhaps in Mendelsohn's exaggerated typology where the heavy accusation of "guilt," rather than responsibility with less criminal culpability, was recommended.

Correlation between the age of the victim and the criminal's attitude after the crime is neither clear-cut nor well understood. Guilt feelings have been expressed by the offender most often in cases where the victim was in the age group of 31 to 40. The criminal felt that his crime was justified mainly in cases in which the victim was 21 to 30 years old. The offender seemed to feel indifference after his crime if his victim was 51 or older or under 21.

Gillies, however, found that the criminals he studied failed completely to voice "any regret for their actions, any sympathy for the victim or any concern for the victim's family."[128]

Some attempts have been made to see how far an offender is prepared to go to compensate his victim. In Schafer's sample, inmates' positive or negative attitudes toward restitution were shown in only 88 cases: in 19 cases of criminal homicide, in 22 cases of aggravated assault, and in 47 cases of violent theft. Attitudes toward compensation, as classified in accordance with the three types of crime, the sex of the offender, and whether positive or negative, are as follows:

1. In criminal homicide (19 cases), 15 males and 3 females expressed a positive attitude, and only 1 male gave a negative response.
2. In aggravated assaults (22 cases), 10 males and 2 females expressed a positive attitude, and 9 males and 1 female expressed a negative attitude.
3. In thefts with violence (47 cases), 24 males and 2 females expressed a positive attitude, and 20 males and 1 female expressed a negative attitude.

The above data, expressed in percentages and projected to each type of crime, is as follows:

	POSITIVE	NEGATIVE
Criminal homicide	94.7%	5.3%
Aggravated assault	54.5%	45.5%
Theft with violence	55.4%	44.6%

These figures indicate that the overwhelming majority of those who committed some form of criminal homicide wished that they could make some reparation. Among those sentenced for aggravated assault, a much smaller proportion (slightly over half) felt obliged to do something for their victim: the rest apparently felt that their debt was due only to the state. Among those who committed robbery or burglary, again only somewhat over half of the offenders felt they had some obligation to the victim; the rest could perceive no legal, moral, ethical, or social link with the victim.

In the course of the interviews involving criminal homicide cases, many of them with prisoners soon to be executed, the impression was gained that their feelings of guilt, involving self-devaluation and apprehension and leading to their preparedness to do something good for the victim's family, grew out of a fear of the penal consequences. It was felt that their proximity to death, to be suffered in the name of human justice, changed their experience-evaluating and behavior-selecting attitudes toward right and away from wrong. Not punishment as pain, but a realization of the limit placed on their natural life seemed to relate them to social obligations, reparation for their wrongdoing among them. However, this was not experienced by inmates who were sentenced for aggravated assault or theft with violence. These offenders, at least many of them, did not appear to be intropunitive and apparently could not understand—and thus could not accept—their functional responsibility. Their orientation was such that they could not understand their wrongdoing in terms of social relationships, not even in terms of the victim. Their understanding of incarceration seemed limited to what they viewed as merely a normative wrong that has to be paid to the agencies of criminal justice, but to no one else. Their reluctance to go beyond this isolated and narrow attitude was not due to some deviant logic, but to a lack of understanding of the referent factors of their crime.[129]

In 1958 Stephen Schafer proposed a kind of victim compensation to be performed by the offender. Some fifteen years later, in the early 1970s, his recommendation for corrective restitution received practical attention and application, and is now being experimented with in Minnesota and Massachusetts, among other places. It is hoped that corrective restitution will change both the victim's and the criminal's attitude after the crime: the victim's toward a better understanding of the offender and of the administration of criminal law; and the offender's toward re-recognizing his victim (who almost disappeared in the proceedings of the legal administration) and toward correcting himself.

Previous Criminal Record

The hardened criminal and the innocent victim are popularly believed to be the participants in crime. If James V. Bennett is correct in suggesting that more than half of the prison population returns within five years after being discharged,[130] it is possible that more than half of the victims are attacked by recidivist criminals, and less than half by first offenders. According to the "careers in crime" study by the FBI, of 134,938 federal offenders, three out of every four were repeaters;[131] this would reduce criminal contacts of victims with first offenders to one quarter of the cases.

Wolfgang supports the contention that "criminal homicide offenders have a strong proclivity for engaging in crimes of violence or of personal assault rather than in crimes of an acquisitive nature."[132] Gibson and Klein arrived at different results; among their repeaters, "almost all had been convicted of larceny or breaking and entering" and about a quarter of these had also committed an offense against the person. They suggest that capital murderers are mostly thieves "who kill in pursuit of criminal activities."[133] Among the violent criminals he studied, Schafer found that in cases of a single previous offense, 66.7 percent of the offenders had committed different types of crime; but all those with four previous crimes on their record had been sentenced for the same type of crime each time.[134] Gillies found a history of violence in a minority of the murderers he studied; most of their previous records contained offenses of a nonviolent nature. None had been previously charged with murder.[135] This suggests caution in setting up patterns of crime repetition; however, there are reliable indications that there are criminals with a tendency to commit the same or similar offenses.

Data about the victim are scarce, and our information about his criminal record is particularly scarce. In homicide and other violent crimes, it is estimated that close to half of the victims have a criminal record containing one or more offenses against the person. This suggests that the violent personal clash often occurs among those who are inclined toward violent acts, and that it is not at all rare for the victim himself to be a motivating factor in his own suffering.

Patterns of Time

The time of the day, the day of the week, the season of the year —in other words, the temporal aspects of crime—may shed some light on risks of victimization. The effect of "time" on crime is not new to criminology. Temperature, climate, and change of season are among the oldest factors in the study of crime, and the effect of man's physical environment on criminality engaged the attention of some thinkers long before criminology as a discipline became known and recognized. Guerry[136] and Adolphe Quetelet[137] were among early investigators who were interested in the relationship between morality and climate, and they related French crimes against the person to places where warmer weather is prevalent. Leone Levi's survey in England reached a similar conclusion, and found that crimes against the person are more numerous in summer than in winter.[138] George von Mayr's reference to the "influence of nature,"[139] Enrico Ferri's[140] and William Douglas Morrison's[141] "cosmic" consideration of crime, Meyer's "tellurionic" interpretations,[142] and Gaedeken's speculation about the "physico-chemical influence of meteorologic agents" on crime[143] prompted a number of studies on the connection between crime and specific weeks, months, seasons, and climate.[144]

The FBI *Crime Reports* suggest that murder follows a seasonal pattern and occurs more frequently in the summer months, except for a high rate in December. Similar patterns can be observed regarding forcible rape and robbery, but without a flare-up in winter months.[145] Wolfgang's Philadelphia findings regarding the high frequency of criminal homicides in summer and on Saturdays, and his reference to "the most lethal hours" between 8:00 P.M. and 2:00 A.M. give empirical support to longstanding assumptions.[146]

Schafer's Florida findings revealed significant correlation between the time of day when a crime is committed and the sex of the offender.[147] The division of the day into three eight-hour periods was an arbitrary research decision: daytime, 6:00 A.M. to 2:00 P.M.; evening, 2:00 P.M. to 10:00 P.M.; night, 10:00 P.M. to 6:00 A.M. It indicated that males commit most of their violent crimes at night and that females commit fewer violent crimes in the evening hours. Males commit violent crimes at night three times more often than in the daytime and almost fifteen times more often than in the evening. Generally, criminals of both sexes appear to be "least criminal" in the evening. Victimizations, naturally, show corresponding patterns. The male victim is more often attacked at night, and the female victim is least often attacked in the evening.

Similarly, statistics for the two sexes do not concur as to the day of the week. Male criminals commit violent crimes mainly on weekdays, and more than twice as frequently as on weekends. However, females commit violent crimes mainly on weekends, mostly on

Sundays and least of all on Fridays. One may speculate that females are victimized more often on weekdays than males. Sunday turned out to be the day when males are most often victims of violent crimes, as opposed to a rather low proportion of female victims.

It has been observed that males commit most of their violent crimes in winter (December–February) and in the spring (March–May). However, females commit most of their violent crimes in the autumn (September–November). Victimizations correspond.

An attempt has been made to correlate the age of the offender with the time of the day when the crime was committed. It was found that all age groups prefer the night for violent crimes; but those in the age group of 21 to 30 prefer the night hours for crime more than do other age groups. The highest relative frequency of violent daylight crimes is committed by offenders who are 31 to 50 years old. Generally, the participation of the various age groups in violent crimes as projected to each period of the day is in proportion to the growth and decline of physical energy. The frequency of violent crimes at night by criminals who are 30 or under is rather high. However, over this age the frequency seems to shift to daytime crimes, and it shifts back to nighttime crimes only after the age of 61.

Members of the age group of 21 to 30 commit most of their violent crimes on weekdays, but they head the list for frequency on all days. Criminal activities on weekdays are proportionately less as one moves from younger to older age groups. Except for those who are 61 and older, the older the offender the more likely his crime will be committed during a weekend.

Crime also varies by age groups according to the season. The strongest relationship appears between criminals of 21 to 30 and violent crimes committed in the winter (December–February). The weakest relationship appears between the oldest age group (61 and older) and violent crimes committed in the autumn (September–November). The age group of 21 to 30 heads the rate of violent crime for all seasons. The next highest rate is for those in the 31 to 40 age group for the spring (March–May) and the summer (June–August). For the age group of 21 and under, the autumn and the winter show the highest rates of violent crimes.

Time is also a selective factor in crime types. In the daytime, most violent crimes are aggravated assaults, with a relatively higher frequency than in any other period of the day. This might be explained by the greater opportunity people have to meet each other, leading in turn to more possibilities for clashes and arguments. Only slightly less frequent than aggravated assault is the daytime frequency of theft with violence, but with almost the lowest relative frequency as compared with other periods of the day. Criminal homicide ranks last for frequency in the daytime.

Evening hours seem to favor homicide. As compared with aggravated assault, the more often criminal homicide is committed in the evening, the less often it is committed in the daytime. At night criminal homicides, at least in relative terms, seem to decline, almost to the level of the daytime cases. At night robberies and burglaries are the most frequent among violent offenses; they occur almost twice as often as homicides.

In an absolute sense, all three violent types of crime (criminal homicide, aggravated assault, and theft with violence) are mostly committed at night. The evening hours appeared to be the most peaceful; no one quite knows why this is so. One may conjecture that in Florida, where Schafer conducted his research, "evening-hours" means the shortest period of the day, an even shorter period than in the northern United States, and this rather brief transition from daylight to darkness does not offer very many opportunities for crime.

Research tells us that weekdays favor the commission of robberies and burglaries, whereas on Saturdays and Sundays the incidence of aggravated assault is highest. Criminal homicides are concentrated on holidays. The fact that places of business are open may encourage the weekday incidence of thefts with violence, and the fact of greater contact between people during weekends may increase the frequency of aggravated assaults. But these are matters of speculation.

In every period of the day, on every day of the week, and in every season of the year, the stranger is most often the victim. This fits in with all overall categories of general criminal statistics. During any period of the day, violent crimes occur against the spouse more often than against other relatives; and during the evening hours spouses are victims of violent crimes more often than persons in any other relationship, except "strangers." This may lead to the assumption that the evening is the time of day when married people have the greatest opportunity to argue with each other, a situation that may be aggravated by the pile-up of tension from the day's work.

Although violent crimes against the spouse have their highest incidence on weekdays (Monday through Thursday), Saturday is the day when more violent crimes are committed against the spouse than against persons (except strangers) in any other relationship. On Saturdays, there is probably no outside tension to divert married people from potential arguments within the family circle, and thus, because they may be more concentrated, quarrels may lead to violent outbreaks. Why spouse victimizations seem to occur mostly in the autumn is not known. Violent victimization of children occurs most often in the spring and in the summer.

The victim's occupation has no statistically significant correlation with the time when a crime is committed. In general, it was observed that most daytime crimes of violence, at least in Schafer's research findings, are committed against unemployed persons. This is probably because the crimes are aggravated assaults in which property aspiration plays little or no part. In daytime offenses with violence, semiskilled and unskilled persons occupy second place in the incidence of victimization, and persons in clerical and sales occupations occupy third place. In evening crimes, semiskilled and unskilled persons are most frequently victimized; managers, officials, and proprietors come next, followed by those in clerical and sales occupations. Nighttime crimes, like evening crimes, are directed mainly against semiskilled and unskilled persons; these are followed by unemployed persons, and individuals in clerical and sales positions.

Projection of the seasons to occupational categories reflects the important functional period of each occupation. Professional and technical persons have their highest victim-risk in the autumn and in winter months. Farmers seem to face the peak of potential victimization in the autumn. Managers, officials, and proprietors have their highest victim-risk in winter months—about twice as much risk as in the summer. Clerical and sales people are in danger of victimization mostly in the winter. Craftsmen and foremen have their highest victim-risk in the spring. Semiskilled and unskilled individuals are victimized mainly in the winter.

Findings for the day, week, and season combined indicate that the strongest relationship exists between nighttime and weekday violent crimes, and the weakest between evening and Sunday crimes. In general, weekdays had the highest frequency of daytime violent offenses, more than three times as many as weekend days. Weekday crimes also led in frequency of incidence in the evening hours and at night.

Nighttime crimes lead among all crimes in any season, but violent crimes at night are most frequent in the winter months. In this respect, the least victim-risk occurs in autumn evening hours. As mentioned before, weekday crimes dominate in all seasons; yet in the spring and in the autumn months crimes on Saturdays, and in the summer and winter months crimes on Fridays, follow in frequency those committed on Mondays through Thursdays.

Whether or not anyone is with the offender at the time of the crime is an important factor. Most crimes are committed by one person acting alone, and this proved to be true for all periods of the day. If the criminal had one partner, violent crimes were more frequent in the evening hours and at night. However, if the offender had five partners or more, they were most likely to occur in the daytime. This may indicate that gangs and other criminal organizations do not favor the night. This seems to be a rapidly developing trend, mainly in crimes against property; apparently modern safety and security devices create difficulties for the underworld so they tend to prefer a quick daytime holdup as safety and security measures are often neglected during the daytime. In warmer seasons, that is, in late spring and in the summer, most violent crimes are committed by the offender acting alone or with one partner. In colder seasons, that is, in late autumn and winter, most violent offenses seem to be committed by five or more criminal participants.

Whether anyone is with the victim at the time of a violent crime is significantly related to victim-risk. Most violent crimes are committed at night against solitary, lonely victims; apparently this happens some sixteen times more often than during the evening hours and three times more often than in daylight hours. Daytime crimes against victims who are in the company of three or more people occur more often than at night. The lonely victim is an easy prey of the criminal on weekdays and on Saturdays, primarily in the winter months. The lowest victim-risk is in the summer months if the victim is in the company of four or more.

Spatial Aspects of the Victim-Risk

The geographical and spatial aspects of violent crimes offer important clues for potential victimizations. What is the size of the area, in terms of its population, where the crime was committed? What is the type of the crime area? Is it a suburb, a residential locality, or a business district? Does the violent crime take place on a main street, a back srteet, or was it committed at some deserted place? If the crime was committed "inside," did it take place in a house or an apartment, in a bar, in a shop or a store, or at another interior locale? Where is the residence of the victim and that of the offender with respect to the distance from the place of the crime? Although we are approaching the point where all places at all times are "dangerous," and all of us, being potential victims, should be alert at all times, all these factors play significant roles in, and suggest the chances of, victim-risks.

The relatively high frequency of criminal homicides and aggravated assaults in small communities, as reported by Schafer, supports the longstanding speculation that intense and frequent contact among people increases the likelihood of clashes. Frequency of crimes against property is lower in small communities, however, because they do not offer much opportunity for this type of crime; moreover, smaller groups have tighter control. Robberies and burglaries increase markedly when communities reach a population of 10,000, and are greatest in communities with a population of 100,000 or over. This supports evidence to the effect that criminals increase their opportunities by moving to larger communities. The bigger the community, the looser the contact of people with each other; this may explain the lesser tensions and the lower rate of criminal homicides and assaults in places with a large population. The increasing trend in all types of crime in conjunction with increases in population indicates that overall opportunities for the criminal have increased, and that the development of more crimes, criminals, and victims is mathematically probable.

An extremely strong and statistically significant correlation has been observed between the different types of violent crime and the type of area in which the crime is committed. Theft with violence sharply dominates in business areas of the suburbs, and even more so in the case of downtown business districts, where valuable property is concentrated. It follows that there would be a relatively lower incidence of criminal homicides and aggravated assaults in main business districts, and a somewhat higher rate of them in nonresidential parts of suburbs where businesses are in operation. In these areas many offenses against the person are only incidental to the crimes against property.

Criminal homicides and aggravated assaults are relatively higher in residential areas. This can be explained by the close contact of people with each other and the resulting tension, and perhaps also by the relative absence of opportunities for crimes against property, into which some criminal effort might otherwise have gone. If aggravated assaults stand out moderately in business districts, where property crimes predominate, this suggests the possibility of frequent arguments and tensions in the course of everyday work.

Most violent crimes are committed in main streets, yet most of these crimes are robberies and burglaries. In backstreet crimes more aggravated assaults show up. Deserted places seem to favor homicidal attacks and robberies. The rather high incidence of theft with violence in deserted places is not well understood, except if the theft is from the person (and not from business premises).

In pinpointing victim-risk, it has been observed that no places are more frequently the objects of theft with violence than shops and stores, and no places can rank as high as family houses and apartments in the incidence of criminal homicides. Shops and stores, obviously because they offer an abundance of opportunities, are favored for burglaries and robberies. Family houses and apartments, probably because they permit tensions to build up without being witnessed by outsiders, are most frequently the scene of emotionally engendered homicides. The street seems to be the place for violent thefts rather than for crimes against the person. Bars, most likely because of the effect of alcohol, are predominantly the locale for aggravated assault (but not for homicide). Robberies are more prevalent in bars than murders.

In communities of all sizes, the least amount of crime occurs during evening hours, and night involves the highest victim-risk. Violent attacks in residential areas occur mainly at night, while in business districts most victimization occurs in daylight; the opportunities open to the criminal in each instance make this logical. Nighttime crimes lead in frequency, and the lowest victim-risk obtains in the evening hours, regardless of the locale of the crime—except in the case of crimes committed in back streets, where violent crimes in the evening hours have a relatively high frequency.

In communities with a population of 50,000 or less, most crimes with violence are committed on Saturdays, and even the Sunday rate is higher than the Friday rate. In cities with a larger population, Friday crimes increase and overtake Saturday and Sunday crimes in frequency. Again, however, the incidence of violent crimes on weekdays (except Friday) is sharply higher in all communities and all areas than that of any weekend day. On Sundays and holidays most businesses are closed and this is why the crime rate is lower on weekdays in business districts. However, the relatively high proportion of violent crimes, mainly offenses against the person, in residential areas on Saturdays and Sundays is explained by the fact that people are at home on these days. The degree of contact between people should also explain why there are fewer main-street crimes on weekends. There is an outstanding crime rate for deserted places on weekend days, mainly Saturdays. By the same token, it is understandable that shops and stores are the setting for violent crimes more often on Fridays, and even more often on Saturdays, than on Sundays, and that violent crimes are committed in family houses and apartments mostly on Sundays. The high proportion of violent crimes in bars on Fridays can be explained by the fact that it is a payday and also a time when the week's work responsibilities have ended.

As to crime in terms of seasons and population: in the smallest towns (population of 5,000 and under) and in the largest (population of 100,000 and over) most violent crimes are committed during the winter. In communities between 5,000 and 100,000, most violent crimes are committed during the spring. In larger communities, the summer months have the weakest correlation with crimes with violence and one might connect this finding with the fact that vacations temporarily reduce population. More violent crimes are committed in business districts than in residential areas, except in the autumn. Main streets and back streets lead in violent crimes, primarily in the winter; deserted places lead in the spring and in the autumn. Weather conditions can explain the low frequency of violent offenses in deserted places in the winter months, but why the frequency is low in the summer is not known. Again, weather conditions may explain the sharply higher frequency of violent crimes in family houses, apartments, and bars in the colder months of the year.

Distance Considerations

Computations have been made of the correlation between the distance (in approximate miles) from the criminal's residence to the scene of the crime with the distance (in approximate miles) from the victim's residence. This computation led to significant findings concerning victim-risks. When the victim lived at the place of the crime, in 61.5 percent of the cases the criminal lived there, too; in 15.4 percent, the criminal lived one to three miles away. When the victim lived less than a mile away, and when the victim lived one to three miles away, the criminal lived at the same distance in each case. In crimes where the victim lived three to ten miles away, in 66.7 percent of the cases the criminal, too, lived three to ten miles away; in only 33.3 percent of the cases did he live more than 10 miles away. When the victim lived more than 10 miles away, the criminal, also, in 66.7 percent of the cases, lived at a similar distance; in only 33.3 percent of the cases did he live nearer (three to ten miles). This indicates that, as a general rule, both criminal and victim live at about the same distance from the scene of the crime; at least this is what the Florida research reveals.

Correlation between the age of the victim and the distance from the criminal's residence to the scene of the crime had no statistical significance. The strongest relationship appeared between victims in the age group of 31 to 40 and criminals who lived three to ten miles from the scene of the crime, and between victims in the age group of 51 to 60 and criminals who lived more than 10 miles away. Also insignificant was the correlation between the age of the victim with the distance from his home to the scene of the crime. The strongest relationship appeared between victims under 21 and their residence as the scene of the crime. All of these victims in the research were victimized in their own homes. Also, the crime was committed in the victim's home in all those cases in which he was 41 to 50 years old. About half of the victims in the age groups of 31 to 40 and of 61 and over were attacked in their own homes.

When spatial factors are considered in connection with the relationship of the victim to his criminal, victim-risks are indicated. In general, in agreement with all other observations, the stranger (third person) is the one who is victimized most frequently, regardless of the location of the scene of the crime. This is especially true of violent crimes committed in business districts; this is logical in view of the large number of property crimes in such areas. Residential areas have a rather high rate of criminal violence against the spouse and against friends. In fact, most violent crimes against the spouse are committed in residential areas, and only a small proportion occur in the suburbs and in business districts. However, most violent crimes against the offender's own child seemed to be committed in the suburbs.

With respect to violent crime, a clear distinction between the suburbs and residential areas (as defined below) is extremely difficult, if indeed the distinction can be made at all. A residential area is considered here as a place that has few, if any, businesses and that is predominantly middle class. By a suburb is meant the outskirts of a city, with a mixed class stratification, and with a substantial number of businesses located among residences. Without a closer investigation of the people themselves, such as the middle-class attitude toward violence against the spouse, or the lower-class attitude toward violence against one's own child, no trustworthy data can be derived from the findings.

Violent crimes against persons who have any relationship with the offender take place most frequently on main streets. Deserted places have the weakest correlation with crimes committed against friends; violent crimes against friends are probably committed so much under the pressure of emotion that they do not involve the planning that is often required for crimes committed in deserted places. The high percentage of violent crimes against the spouse that are committed in family houses and apartments clearly indicates that most personal dramas of this kind take place in the home. The same applies to violent crimes against the criminal's own child.

Wolfgang attempted to investigate the specific place in the house or apartment where criminal homicides take place, and found that data of this kind in police files are more accessible than any other information. He suggests that "the bedroom has the dubious honor of being the most dangerous room in the home," and that the kitchen and the living room are to an equal extent the next most dangerous.[148] The specific location of a crime within a house or an apartment is mainly significant in establishing the flow of events leading to the crime and in tracing the motivation of both criminal and victim.

The Methods of Crime

The more advanced our technology, the greater variety of methods are at the disposal of the criminal. Today we have to cope with many more criminal methods than we did, say, a century ago. There are many new tools, instruments, and machines that are used not only for the comfort and benefit of the members of society (that is, the potential victims), but are also used to facilitate crimes against them. The automobile is not only used to rush a doctor to a criminally wounded person but is also used by the criminal for an efficient getaway. Gloves are used not only to protect the hands in cold weather, but also to conceal fingerprints.

In the matter of crimes with violence, new methods are utilized mainly in crimes against property; traditional methods are mostly used in aggravated assaults and criminal homicides. In Gillies' study, the deaths of seventy victims resulted from sharp and blunt instruments, shooting, strangulation or asphyxiation, or barbiturate poisoning.[149] Gibson and Klein list almost the same methods of murder.[150] Wolfgang lists stabbing, shooting, and beating as methods. He lists penknife, knife, switchblade, pistol and revolver, rifle and shotgun, fists, feet, and blunt instruments as weapons for killing.[151] The FBI *Uniform Crime Reports* list as weapons used in criminal homicides the gun, cutting or stabbing, a blunt object (club, hammer, or similar weapon), hands and other parts of the body (resulting in strangling and beatings), poison, explosives, and others (drownings and arson, for example).[152]

In Schafer's Florida investigation "bare hands" as the method of crime was found mostly in violent offenses committed for profit, in crimes committed under the influence of alcohol, and in crimes committed during an emotional outburst. Skeleton keys and similar tools were not used in offenses with violence when "smoother" or "intellectual" methods were preferred. Guns were used primarily in crimes for profit, or if the offender acted under emotional pressure, and about three times more often than in cases where the crime was motivated by financial need or alcohol. Cuttings, stabbings, and use of a blunt object proved to be typical of emotional crimes in which the criminal used the first weapon he could get his hands on. In the overall picture the gun is used most often.[153]

There is a marked difference between males and females both in methods and in instruments used in violent crimes. Wolfgang suggests, referring only to criminal homicides, that females kill during domestic quarrels, "which frequently occur in kitchens while they are preparing meals"; thus it is not unlikely that they use cutting or stabbing instruments. However, males use blunt instruments or their fists alone, and "beat their victims to death nine to ten times more often than do female offenders."[154] Schafer found that only a slightly higher percentage of females over males were victimized barehanded; however, this was for all types of violent crime.[155] In general, in crimes with violence, the male prefers the gun, and the female favors cutting and stabbing. This may indicate the victim-risk of the different sexes.

The preference for guns in violent crimes can be observed in all relationships between victim and criminal. Attacks against the spouse are made mainly with a gun or a stabbing and cutting instrument; also, barehanded attacks outnumber attacks with a blunt object. In the family, the spouse seems to be the only one who is victimized barehanded. The criminal uses a gun or a blunt instrument when attacking his child. Strangers (third persons) are attacked in all conceivable ways, but the majority are victims of shootings.

In all violent crimes (criminal homicide, aggravated assault, burglary and robbery) the gun is used most, followed by cutting and stabbing, and then by other methods. The gun is used in most cases during any period of the day and on any day of the week. Blunt objects are used minimally during evening hours. Most barehanded violent crimes occur in the daytime. Cutting and stabbing instruments are used mainly on weekdays and on Saturdays during the weekend. The gun is used more than other weapons during every season of the year, but is used most frequently in the summer and winter months. Barehanded crimes seem to occur mostly in the autumn. However, the correlation of criminal methods and instruments to different seasons is not well understood.

The method or weapon used may reflect the victim's attitude in crime. Since present data are derived only from cases of violent crime, and one of them is theft with violence, it is understandable that in many instances the victim was absent, and thus could not evidence any particular attitude toward the crime. In most barehanded crimes the victim resists, and this would indicate the victim's hope to overcome the criminal whenever, at least apparently, he is not paralyzed by the weapon used. In most cases in which the offender used a gun, the victim was passive. In 75 percent of the crimes in which a cutting or stabbing instrument was used, the victim proved to be provocative, perhaps as the result of a close, heated, person-to-person argument. The provocation explains the choice of weapon, since usually a knife or a similar object is close at hand when provoked emotions demand immediate action. The use of blunt objects was also victim-provoked, but with less frequency; in many instances the victim was passive.

In most violent crimes the victim's postcrime attitude has proved to be retributive in nature. In many violent crimes against family members, the relationship between the crime participants should explain the presence of a lenient or forgiving attitude. Violent crimes against family members are most often committed barehanded or with stabbing or cutting weapons. The use of a gun in many cases leads the victim's postcrime attitude to passivity, in some cases even to slight leniency.

The Significance of the Early Empirical Studies

Promising as they are, the above-mentioned attempts to approach and understand the structure of crime through the victim's participation have not provided more than the beginnings of a framework, the first steps in a neglected aspect of the crime problem, in which a rather wide range of interrelations and personal interactions between criminal and victim often occur. Their main contribution to the understanding of the victim's role in crime is to lead the way toward study of a particular area of criminology, in which victim-risks, victim provocations, victim-precipitation, and victim-participation, and the characteristics of the victim of crime can more definitely be examined. The study of victimology is meant to broaden the universal understanding of crime in terms of the functional responsibility of the lawbreaker, as well as that of the victims. The insistence that this new, or, better, *revived* aspect of crime should be a new science or an independent or separate discipline does not seem to have survived its first sympathetic acceptance. The very fact that the victim's role as a sufferer of, or a participant in, a crime should be studied in itself supports the objections against separating the victim from the general crime problem. It is generally agreed that our lack of knowledge about the victim and his relationship with the criminal makes the understanding of crime incomplete. The gap, where criminal-victim relationships and the victim's functional responsibility should appear, is beginning to be filled.

A widely-held belief, which developed as a result of the trend toward recognizing the victim's importance, interprets the criminal's and his victim's joint presence in crime as a comprehensive dual behavior that should stem from the objectivized, formalistic-legalistic skeleton structure of the crime concept. Crime, and the criminal's and his victim's responsibility, should be seen in its functional dynamics. An all-dimensional view of crime, where the participants' function defines their responsibilities, can hardly accept the criminal's behavior and the victim's behavior as two distinct and separate forms of conduct. Even at the present stage of knowledge, it is generally recognized that the victim is not simply a part of the evidence, that he is not merely the cause of, or the reason for, criminal proceedings—without whom or without whose injury, harm, or disadvantage the machinery of criminal justice could not operate. Rather, he is a part of the crime, often playing an esoteric and not an exoteric role.

In fact, everyone, regardless of age, sex, race, occupation, social stratification, or other classification, is exposed to the possibility of a criminal attack of some kind. In other words, all members of a society are potential victims. But, and this is what the study of criminal-victim relationships is aiming at, not all victims are wholly passive sufferers of the attacking criminal, and the terms "offender" and "victim" fundamentally designate only a legal position. Many offenders are offended by the victim, or, better, many victims victimize the offender; thus, the doer-sufferer distinction does not mean the exclusive doing of one party and the suffering of the other. This mutuality of doing and suffering between the participants in a crime may appear in any criminal offense. However, the composition and proportion of activity and passivity vary according to the influence of a multitude of interplaying factors, such as the type of crime, the personalities of the offender of the victim, their relationship with each other, and the circumstances of the criminal act. These and other factors can be analyzed only in each individual case. The sufferer's doing—in other words, the victim's activity—is not necessarily precipitative in nature; it can be either more forceful and decisive in determining the offender's crime or less forceful and indeterminate, thus merely facilitating, shaping, or molding the crime, or increasing the offender's motivation.

The significance of the sufferer's doing—and the combination of doing and suffering as the functional substances of crime commission—most of the time cannot be clearly seen or well understood, and the victim's role in a crime, if any, is not only largely ignored in both judicial and criminological consideration, but is also frequently too deeply hidden to be detected. One may be justified in thinking that a great deal of positive victim participation is not known: because investigations do not go into areas that might reveal them, or because there is no investigative technique that can reach them. It is assumed, however, that the more physical activity is involved in a crime, the better are the chances for observing the victim's eventual contribution to it. This is one of the reasons why, at least in early empirical or theoretical victimological studies, most research is devoted to violent crimes. Such crimes are more difficult to conceal, and the criminal's extrovert aggression and visible physical force may open up an opportunity for making the victim more visible not only as a sufferer but also as a doer. Violent crimes are selected for research also because of the embryonic state of this region of criminology, and because they establish the framework for exploratory experimentation that concentrates exclusively on criminal-victim relationships.

The renewal of interest in the victim does not mean that his role and importance in criminal proceedings and his involvement in efforts to understand the crime problem are in fact already revived. Rather it indicates that a beginning has been made toward this revival, which should lead to the understanding of criminal, victim, and society in terms of their functional responsibilities. However, in order to achieve the desired goal, we need a better understanding of the goal, more theoretical thinking about the aspirations of victimology, and more research (based on theories).

Empirical Studies after the Beginnings of Victimological Studies

Victimization Studies

After the pioneering studies in victimology, the President's Commission on Law Enforcement and Administration of Justice made efforts to stimulate further investigations.[156] Although it referred to the criminal-victim relationships and to the responsibility of the crime participants by stating that both the part the victim can play in the criminal act and the part he could have played in preventing it are often overlooked, the Commission actually discussed "victimizations," which is hardly more than what the conventional crime studies do that offer only demographic data and leave the theoretical speculation to the reader. Their concentration has been on the "victimization risk," rather than on the characteristics of the relationships and the attending degree of functional responsibility.

It has been shown by the Commission's work that rather striking variations "in the risk of victimization" for different types of crime appear among different income levels in the population. Forcible rape, robbery, and burglary are clearly concentrated in the lowest income group and decrease steadily at higher income levels. The "victimization rate" for women is highest in the 20 to 29 age group, and it is concentrated in rape and robbery; for men it is highest in the 30–39 age class, with concentration in burglaries; and it is highest in aggravated assaults in lower age groups. The Commission admitted that unfortunately no national statistics are available on relationships between the criminal and his victim (we still do not have such statistics available), and possibly criminal homicide may be the only exception. For the latter, the most striking fact that has been pointed out is the correlation in race between victim and offender: Blacks are most likely to assault Blacks, and whites are most likely to assault whites. The Commission made also clear that it is very difficult to discover the exact extent to which businesses and organizations are the victims of crime.

Although, as the Commission's Task Force Report asserted, "information about victims and their relationships to offenders is recorded in the case files of the police and other criminal justice agencies, it is rarely used for systematic study of those relationships or the risks of victimization."[157] Only the pioneering studies—or even largely unrelated studies—have been mentioned in the footnotes of the Report, and close to nothing has been voiced, and even less has been done, for designing and establishing victim statistics that would serve purposes other than simply the indication of victim risks. The continued emphasis on victimization risks (the risk of crime) in present day victimization studies, may mean the acceptance of the state of crime as is—the indication being that we should protect ourselves against it and learn to adjust to the world of criminals. This seems to be characteristic in the victimization studies of the Law Enforcement Assistance Administration's sponsored surveys on Dayton, Ohio and San Jose, California,[158] among others,[159] as well as surveys on the United States in general.[160] Some even have glossaries that clearly admit that "victimization" is "a specific criminal act." They also have explanatory prefaces that explain that this nationwide program of continuing surveys gauges the extent to which persons, households, and businesses have been victimized. They appear to amount to extended and more detailed editions of the Federal Bureau of Investigation's yearly *Uniform Crime Reports*.

This misconception of what "victimology" really means has probably originated in the misunderstanding of Philip H. Ennis' study, which is not a true victimological study, but is still closer to it than any studies made by his successors.[161] The primary goal of Ennis, as he stated it,[162] was "to measure the amount" of crime, yet he attempted it through promising interviews with victims. These interviews sought to establish the nature of the crime, where and how it took place, the extent and nature of losses, injuries or damage, the notification of the police, or reasons for failing to report the incident to the police, the judicial outcome of the case, and whatever descriptions there were available about the offender; the attitudes of the victims were also probed. In other words, he not only attempted to answer questions such as "how much crime?" or "how much loss?" or what is the distribution of crime, but also he tried to establish the place of the crime, the racial relationship between the victim and his criminal, the circumstances of notifying the law enforcement agencies, and the victim's attitudes.

Ennis claimed that Blacks are at least as likely to be victimized by whites as whites are by Blacks. This brought him to the analysis of the more microscopic spatial dimension of the neighborhood. He found that 23 percent of crimes were committed inside the home, 29 percent near the home, 10 percent at other private homes or places, 6 percent inside public buildings (e.g., stores, restaurants), 18 percent outside public places (e.g., streets, parks, beaches), and 14 percent at other places. Among aggravated assaults, for example, inside their own homes 50 percent white and 40 percent of nonwhite females were the perpetrators. Of Ennis's many findings, it might be worth noting that where the victim did not notify the police, some did not want to take time, some were afraid of reprisal, others were too confused, but the great majority of the victims had a negative view toward the effectiveness of the law enforcement agencies: they felt that the police could do nothing about the matter or that they would not want to be bothered. In general, it has been concluded that:

- Blacks are far more critical of the police than whites;
- the higher the victim's income the more favorable his view of the police;
- among the higher income Blacks the criticism against the police is harsher;
- sex differences are relatively minor, yet the Black women appeared to be more critical than the men;
- and it was not clear whether the police should devote their energies toward preventing crime or concentrate on catching criminals.

International Conferences

In addition to a number of victimological studies on a small scale (Koichi Miyazawa established at the Keio University in Tokyo a "victimological institute" with a busy schedule of research), the true impact of the growth of victimology has been indicated by international conventions. In 1970 in Madrid, Spain, at the Sixth International Criminological Congress, a full session, chaired by Stephen Schafer, was devoted to problems of victimology, with contributions of Franco Ferracuti from Italy, Ezzat A. Fattah from Canada, Simha F. Landau from Israel, Joseph Vigh and Endre Károly from Hungary, and others. In September 1973, sponsored by the International Society of Criminology and organized by Israel Drapkin, the First International Symposium on Victimology was held in Jerusalem, Israel, with hundreds of participants from all over the world. The deliberations and resolutions of this First Symposium revealed that there are still a great number of problems and questions that remain unanswered, and further opportunities should be provided for discussing them and for illuminating various aspects of victimology. The First Symposium resolved to hold a

Second International Symposium, organized by Stephen Schafer and sponsored by the International Society of Criminology, in September 1976 in Boston, Massachusetts.

In 1974 in Budapest, Hungary, at the World Congress on Penal Law, organized by the International Association of Penal Law, one of the four major topics was the problem of compensating victims of crime, which provoked stimulating discussions under the chairmanship of the German Hans-Heinrich Jescheck. In 1975 in Bellagio, Italy, Emilio Viano organized a victimological workshop, and for 1977 a Latin American victimology convention is planned; it will be organized by Israel Drapkin. The International Society of Criminology in Paris has created a victimology division to be headed by Stephen Schafer that is to prepare a victimology program for the Eighth International Criminological Congress to be held in 1980 in Rome. This series of international discussions on victimological problems will undoubtedly continue to proliferate.

The First International Symposium on Victimology

One of the many questions raised at the first International Symposium on Victimology was what *victimology* and *victimization* should mean. Beniamin Mendelsohn fought again for the separation of victimology from criminology. In his new notion of "victimity," as he renamed "victimology,"[163] a "science in general" was proposed that referred to a socio-biopsychological phenomenology consisting of either the causes of man's vulnerability, or the "consequences of noxiousness against man, whether the noxious or other factors" are criminal or not, and "whether or not they are subject to jurisdiction." According to Mendelsohn, in this evolutionary phase of victimology, "victimity" means "the whole of the socio-biopsychological characteristics, common to all victims in general, which society wishes to prevent and fight, no matter what their determinants are, criminals or other."[164] Paul Cornil, on the other hand, rightly asserted that victimology is a part of criminology and criminal law.[165] Although it is not evident from the Conclusions and Recommendations of the Symposium, the great majority of the participants supported Cornil's views. These Conclusions and Recommendations say that "broadly speaking" victimology may be defined as a study of the victim in general, yet they emphasize that the Symposium was convened within the framework of criminology,

and it is the discipline of criminology that is enriched by a victimological orientation.

The Conclusions and Recommendations referred to statistical
investigations, which are greatly needed to supplement our quantitative information, and expressed the view that "just as hidden
criminality is a considerable obstacle in criminology, so too is the
hidden victim." One may conclude that *victimization* studies will
make use of crime statistics that include data on the victims of
crime that could help studies in *victimology*. The term *victimization*
is used to refer to the specific incidence, while *victimology* is the
study of and organization of those incidences of victimization into
meaningful data.

It is impossible to list here the great many stimulating papers
that have contributed to the classification of a number of basic
conceptual aspects of victimology;[166] mention should be made,
however, of those voices that have criticized the fashionable term,
victimless crimes. Among others, Hugo Adam Bedau correctly asserted that a category of victimless crimes really does not exist,
there is an inconsistency with which society proceeds in this matter,
and propositions for decriminalizing conducts on the basis of their
"victimless" nature are both irrational and immature.[167] He appeared to be supported by Milo Tyndel who claimed that psychology and law perpetuate the offense although the offender
victimizes himself.[168] Indeed, Hans Joachim Schneider later stated
that "no criminal offense can exist without victim";[169] opposing
Edwin M. Schur,[170] he rightly claims that abortion, homosexuality,
and drug addiction, for example, are not without victims. As Schneider suggested, "there must be always somebody or something
endangered, harmed, or disturbed." Schur, as it appears, has overlooked the self-victimizations (where there *is* a victim) and crimes
against immaterial victims (e.g., society at large, ideology, religion,
and others).

In its Conclusions and Recommendations the Symposium ex-
panded the focus from two-dimensional person-to-person interactions to three-dimensional (e.g., the involvement of a bystander)
and to multidimensional relationships. It was also indicated that
groups, the whole society, or a social system may victimize individuals, or others besides the direct victim himself. Thomas S.
Adler and Jehudit Stern, for example, observed that the descendents
of the Holocaust survivors (victims of concentration camps or other

tortures) proved to be psychologically problematic children, and many of the survivors refrained from having children.[171] Somewhat in the vein of Louis Proal's discussion of the political criminal,[172] Stanley W. Johnston, in his proposition for a "supranational criminology," claimed that it is the right and duty of victims of a national government to seek defense through a "world law"[173]; David Shichor pointed out how the falsely accused defendant is "victim-prone" due to the social effects of publicity, stigmatization, and degradation ceremonies[174]; and Ann C. Burgess and Lytle Holmstrom claimed that in the criminal justice process even the offender can be seen as a victim.[175]

Under the title of "Causes of Victimization" the Symposium dealt with the problem of the victim's responsibility in crime. Steve Nelson and Menachem Amir, for example, found that in hitch-hike rape victimizations the victims' deportment contributed to their being raped: in general, they proved to be submissive, and showed a certain fatalism regarding the rape hazards of hitch-hiking.[176] Inkeri Anttila opened up new horizons in victim-centered criminological research, especially in the areas of policy making determination of the gravity of offenses.[177] Ante Carich called attention to the motive of crime that may be stimulated or provoked by the victim.[178] Pietro Nuvolone discussed the culpability of the victim and the possible circumstances of his provoking the criminal.[179] Jeffrey H. Reiman, in his attempt to define the concept of the victim, raised the question of "who has set the crime in motion."[180] J.E. Mack, in proposing a victim typology, called attention to the victim's "cooperation in risk sharing."[181] The Conclusions and Recommendations, based on the discussions, refuted the concept of the "born-victim," but have maintained the possibility of the victim's precipitating the criminal offense, and unconditionally expressed the view that "concern with victimology and better knowledge of the victim's role can lead to better sentencing."

The Second International Symposium on Victimology

The Second International Symposium on Victimology was held in 1976 in Boston, Massachusetts, and was sponsored by the International Society of Criminology (Paris) and Northeastern University (Boston), with the cooperation of local universities.

This convention, with hundreds of participants from all corners of the world, gave renewed evidence of the significance that victimology plays in criminology. In the discussion of "Conceptual and Substantive Legal Aspects of Victimology," the concept and scope of victimology, victim typologies, the victim in the judicial procedure, and the victims of traffic offenses were subject to deliberations. In another discussion on "Criminal-Victim Relationships," offenses against the person, offenses against property, criminal-victim relationships and the police, and political criminals as victims were covered. In the discussion on "The Victim and the Society," compensation to victims of crime, corporate victimizations, the victim and the mass media of communication, and the victimization of the victim by the society received attention.

The long way toward understanding crime and guilt—not only by studying the criminal, but also his victim—and their functional responsibilities in lawbreaking has begun.

NOTES

1. Hans von Hentig, *The Criminal and His Victim, Studies in the Sociobiology of Crime* (New Haven, 1948).

2. B. Mendelsohn, "The Origin of the Doctrine of Victimology," *Excerpta Criminologica*, Vol. 3, No. 3 (May-June 1963).

3. B. Mendelsohn, "Method to Be Used by Counsel for the Defense in the Researches Made into the Personality of the Criminal," *Revue de Droit Pénal et de Criminologie* (August-October 1937), p. 877.

4. B. Mendelsohn, "Rape in Criminology," *Giustizia Penale* (1940).

5. B. Mendelsohn, "The Victimology," *Études Internationales de Psycho-Sociologie Criminelle* (July-September 1956), pp. 25–26 (essentially the same in French under the title "Une nouvelle branche de la science bio-psycho-sociale, la victimologie").

6. Ibid. (French), pp. 105–07, 108.

7. Hentig, *The Criminal and His Victim*, pp. 404–38.

8. Harry Elmer Barnes and Negley K. Teeters, *New Horizons in Criminology* (3rd ed., Englewood Cliffs, 1959), pp. 595–96.

9. "Profile of a Bank Robber," *FBI Law Enforcement Bulletin,* 34 (November 1965), 22.

10. Walter C. Reckless, *The Crime Problem* (3rd ed., New York, 1961), p. 24.

11. *Task Force Report: Crime and its Impact—An Assessment,* The President's Commission on Law Enforcement and Administration of Justice (Washington, D.C., 1967), p. 80.

12. *The Challenge of Crime in a Free Society,* A Report by the President's

Commission on Law Enforcement and Administration of Justice (Washington, D.C., 1967), p. 22.

13. Ezzat Abdel Fattah, "Towards a Criminological Classification of Victims," *International Criminal Police Review*, 209:162–69, 1967.

14. Thorsten Sellin and Marvin E. Wolfgang, *The Measurement of Delinquency* (New York, 1964).

15. Marvin E. Wolfgang, "Analytical Categories for Research on Victimization," in Armand Mergen-Herbert Schäfer, ed., *Kriminologische Wegzeichen, Festschrift für Hans von Hentig* (Hamburg, 1967), pp. 167–85.

16. Robert A. Silverman, "Victim Typologies: Overview, Critique, and Reformation," in Israel Drapkin and Emilio Viano, eds., *Victimology* (Lexington, Mass., 1974), pp. 55–65.

17. David Landy and Elliot Aronson, "The Influence of the Character of the Criminal and His Victim on the Decisions of Simulated Jurors," in Drapkin and Viano, *Victimology*, pp. 195–204.

18. Gilbert Geis, "Victimization Patterns in White-Collar Crime," *Abstracts* of papers presented and approved by the First International Symposium on Victimology (Jerusalem, 1973), p. 24.

19. Hans Joachim Schneider, *Victimologie: Wissenschaft vom Verbrechensopfer* (Tübingen, 1975), pp. 52–85.

20. Stephen Schafer, *Theories in Criminology: Past and Present Philosophies of the Crime Problem* (New York, 1969), pp. 140–82.

21. M.O. Iturbe, "Victimologia," *Revista Penaly Penitenciario* Ministerio de Educacion y de la Republica Argentina, XXIII, No. 87–90 (1958).

22. Paul Cornil, "Contribution de la 'Victimologie' aux sciences criminologiques," *Revue de Droit Pénal et de Criminologie*, 39 (April 1959), 587–601.

23. Hans von Hentig, "Remarks on the Interaction of Perpetrator and Victim," *Journal of the American Institute of Criminal Law and Criminology*, XXXI (May-June 1940, March-April 1941), 303–9.

24. Jules Simon, "Le Consentement de la victime justifie-t-il les lésions corporelles?" *Revue de Droit Pénal et de Criminologie* (1933), pp. 457–76.

25. Jean Hemard, "Le Consentement de la victime dans le délit de coups et blessures," *Rev. crit. de législ. et jur.* (1933), pp. 292–319.

26. Kahlil Gibran, *The Prophet* (New York, 1935), p. 45.

27. Ernst Roesner, "Mörder und ihre Opfer," *Monatschrift für Kriminologie und Strafrechtsreform*, 29 (1938), 161–85, 209–28.

28. W. Boven, "Délinquants sexuels. Corrupteurs d'enfants. Coupables et victimes," *Schweizer Archiv für Neurologie und Psychiatrie*, 51 (1943), 14–25.

29. Rollin M. Perkins, "The Law of Homicide," *Journal of Criminal Law and Criminology*, 36 (March-April 1946), 412–27.

30. Herbert Wechsler and Jerome Michael, "A Rationale of the Law of Homicide," *Journal of Criminal Law and Criminology*, 36 (March-April 1946), 1280–82.

31. Rhoda J. Milliken, "The Sex Offender's Victim," *Federal Probation*, 14 (September 1950), 22–26.

32. R. Tahon, "Le Consentement de la victime," *Revue de Droit Pénal et de Criminologie* (1951–1952), pp. 323–42.

33. Henri Ellenberger, "Relation psychologiques entre le criminel et la victime," *Revue Internationale de Criminologie et de Police Technique* (1954), pp. 103–21.

34. E. Werner, "Das Opfer des Mordes," *Kriminalistik* (1956), pp. 2–5.

35. Erwin O. Smigel, "Public Attitudes toward Stealing as Related to the Size of the Victim Organization," *American Sociological Review,* 21 (February 1956), 320–27.

36. C. Ehrlich, "Der Betrüger, sein Handwerkszeug und seine Opfer," *Kriminalistik* (October 1957), pp. 365–67.

37. D. Reifen, "Le délinquant sexuel et sa victime," *Revue Internationale de L'Enfant* (1958), pp. 110–24.

38. Hans Schultz, "Kriminologische und Strafrechtliche Bemerkungen zur Beziehung zwischen Täter und Opfer," *Revue Pénale Suisse* (1958), pp. 171–91.

39. C.R. Souchet, "La Victimologie," *La Vie Judiciaire* (December 15, 1958).

40. *Revue de Droit Pénal et de Criminologie* (April 1959).

41. Willy Calewaert, "La Victimologie et l'escroquerie," Ibid., pp. 602–18.

42. Aimée Racine, "L'Enfant victime d'actes contraires aux moeurs commis sur sa personne par ascendant," Ibid., pp. 635–42.

43. L. de Bray, "Quelques Observations sur les victimes des delits de vol," Ibid., pp. 643–49.

44. René Dellaert, "Premiére confrontation de la psychologie criminelle et de la 'victimologie,' " Ibid., pp. 628–34.

45. W.M.E. Noach, "Het Schlachtoffer en de Strafrechtspraak," in W.P.J. Pompe and G. Th. Kempe, eds., *Strafrechtspraak, Criminologische Studiën* (Assen, 1959), pp. 29–41.

46. Leroy G. Schultz, "Interviewing the Sex Offender's Victim," *Journal of Criminal Law, Criminology and Police Science,* 50 (May-June 1959), 448–52.

47. Edwin D. Driver, "Interaction and Criminal Homicide in India," *Social Forces,* 40 (October 1961), 153–58.

48. T.C.N. Gibbens and Joyce Prince, *Child Victims of Sex Offenses* (London, 1963).

49. Albert Günter Hess, "Die Kinderschädung unter besonderer Berücksichtigung der Tatsituation," in Franz Exner, ed., *Kriminalistische Abhandlungen* (Leipzig, 1934), pp. 41–46.

50. W.H. Nagel, "The Notion of Victimology and Criminology," *Excerpta Criminologica,* Vol. 3 (May-June 1963). Similar views appear in the author's "Victimologie," *Tijdschrift voor Strafrecht* (Leiden, 1959), pp. 1–26.

51. Reckless, *The Crime Problem,* pp. 21–22.

52. Ezzat Abdel Fattah, "Quelques Problémes posés á la justice pénale par la victimologie," *International Annals of Criminology* (2nd sem., 1966), pp. 335–61.

53. Marvin E. Wolfgang, *Patterns in Criminal Homicide* (Philadelphia, 1958).

54. Ibid. See Thorsten Sellin's foreword.

55. Evelyn Gibson and S. Klein, "Murder," *Home Office Studies in the Causes of Delinquency and the Treatment of Offenders,* 4 (London, 1961).

56. Hunter Gillies, "Murder in the West of Scotland," *British Journal of Psychiatry,* III (1965), 1087–94.

57. Stephen Schafer, "Criminal-Victim Relationships in Violent Crimes" (unpublished research, *U.S. Department of Health, Education, and Welfare,* July 1, 1965, MH-07058).

58. United Nations, *Criminal Statistics; Standard Classification of Offenses* (New York, March 2, 1959), pp. 6–23.

59. Ronald A. Fisher and Frank Yates, *Statistical Tables, for Biological, Agricultural and Medical Research* (rev. 5th ed., New York, 1957), pp. 126–27.

60. A. Moreau de Jonnés, *Statistique de la Grande Bretagne et de l'Irlande* (Paris, 1938), Vol. II.

61. *Bulletin de la Commission Centrale de Statistique* (Brussels, 1855), Vol. VI.

62. A bibliographical account of 203 works published between 1829 and 1933 can be found in Ernst Roesner, "Bibliographie zum Problem der internationalen Kriminalstatistik," in E. Kohlrausch and Graf W. Gleispach, *Zeitschrift für die gesamte Strafrechtswissenschaft* (Berlin, 1934), Vol. LIII. For other historical information see Thorsten Sellin and Marvin E. Wolfgang, *The Measurement of Delinquency* (New York, 1964), pp. 7–70.

63. "Directives pour l'élaboration des statistiques criminelles dans les divers pays," *Rapport* de la Commission Mixte Constituée par l'Institute Internationale de Statique et la Commission Internationale Pénale et Pénitentiaire, 1937, in Ernest Delaquis, *Recueil de documents en matiére pénale et pénitentiaire,* Vol. XII–3/4 (March 1947), p. 254.

64. Ernst Roesner, "Die internationale Kriminalstatistik in ihrer methodischen Entwicklung," in Friedrich Zahn, *Allgemeines Statistisches Archiv* (Jena, 1932), Vol. 22, No. 1.

65. Wilhelm Sauer, *Kriminalsoziologie* (Berlin, 1933), Vol. I, p. 4.

66. Veli Verkko, "Kriminalstatistiken och den verkliga Brottsligheten," *Nordisk Tidskrift for Strafferet,* Vol. 8 (April 1930).

67. Roland J. Chilton, "Persistent Problems of Crime Statistics" (paper presented to the meetings of the American Sociological Association, Miami, Fla., 1966).

68. "Report," International Statistical Congress, Proceedings of the Fourth Session (London, 1861), p. 217.

69. Franz von Liszt, "Zur Vorbereitung des Strafgesetzentwurfs," *Festschrift für den XXVI. Deutschen Juristentag* (Berlin, 1902), p. 61.

70. Ronald H. Beattie, "Criminal Statistics in the United States—1960," *Journal of Criminal Law, Criminology and Police Science,* 51 (May-June 1960), 61.

71. *Uniform Crime Reports for the United States, 1965,* Federal Bureau of Investigation (Washington, 1966), p. 3.

72. In 1965 the police solution rate nationally was 24.6 percent (see *Uniform Crime Reports, 1965,* pp. 18–20). For all major crime categories lower than cleared cases in 1961, see *Uniform Crime Reports for the United States,* 1961, Federal Bureau of Investigation (Washington, 1962), pp. 13–17. In 1965 in England 39.2 percent of indictable offenses were cleared up, markedly less than in previous years (see *Criminal Statistics, England and Wales,* 1965 (London, 1966), pp. X–XI).

73. *Uniform Crime Reports for the United States, 1965,* pp. 26–27, 106, 152–53.

74. Ibid., p. 105. An estimated population of 75,400,000 has been used for analysis.

75. J. Edgar Hoover, in speech to the American Bar Association, Los Angeles, August 25, 1958. Cited by Barnes and Teeters, *New Horizons in Criminology,* p. 7.

76. "Report on the Cost of Crime," National Commission on Law Observance and Enforcement (Washington, 1931), *Report 12,* pp. 67–70.

77. Edwin H. Sutherland and Donald R. Cressey, *Principles of Criminology* (7th ed., Philadelphia, 1966), p. 23.

78. Barnes and Teeters, *New Horizons in Criminology,* p. 7.

79. Gerhard O.W. Mueller, "Compensation for Victims of Crime: Thought Before Action," *Minnesota Law Review,* 50 (December 1965), 218.

80. Cesare Lombroso and G. Ferrero, *La donna delinquente, la prostituta e la donna normale* (Torino, 1893).

81. Napoleone Colajanni, *La sociologia criminale* (Catania, 1889).

82. Otto Pollak, *The Criminality of Women* (Philadelphia, 1950).

83. Stephen Schafer, "On the Proportions of the Criminality of Women," *Journal of Criminal Law and Criminology,* 39 (May-June 1948), 77–78.

84. Schafer, "Criminal Victim-Relationships," p. 58.

85. Wolfgang, *Patterns,* p. 32.

86. *The Challenge of Crime in a Free Society,* Report of the President's Commission on Law Enforcement and Administration of Justice (Washington, February 1967), p. 39.

87. Schafer, "Criminal-Victim Relationships," p. 59.

88. Wolfgang, *Patterns,* p. 60.

89. Gibson and Klein, "Murder," p. 17.

90. Veli Verkko, *Homicides and Suicides in Finland and Their Dependence on National Character* (Copenhagen, 1951).

91. Hentig, *The Criminal and His Victim,* pp. 406–7.

92. Schafer, "Criminal-Victim Relationships," p. 61.

93. Ibid., pp. 63–64.

94. Wolfgang, *Patterns,* p. 203.

95. Ibid., p. 206.

96. *Report* of the President's Commission on Crime in the District of Columbia (Washington, 1966), pp. 45, 79.

97. Gibson and Klein, "Murder," pp. 19–20.

98. Wolfgang, *Patterns*, p. 213.

99. Schafer, "Criminal-Victim Relationships," pp. 71–73.

100. *The Challenge of Crime in a Free Society*, p. 39.

101. Wolfgang, *Patterns*, p. 65.

102. Pollak, *The Criminality of Women*, p. 156.

103. Gillies, "Murder in the West of Scotland," pp. 1087–88.

104. *The Challenge of Crime in a Free Society*, p. 39.

105. *Uniform Crime Reports*, 1965, p. 106.

106. Gibson and Klein, "Murder," pp. 17–19.

107. Joseph D. Lohman, Lloyd E. Ohlin, and Dietrich C. Reitzes, *Description of Convicted Felons as a Manpower Resource in a National Emergency* (Springfield, Ill.: n.d.), p. 24. (Mimeographed). Quoted by Sutherland and Cressey, *Principles of Criminology*, p. 251.

108. Schafer, "Criminal-Victim Relationships," pp. 84–85.

109. Ruth Shonle Cavan, *Criminology* (3rd ed., New York, 1962), p. 498.

110. Christopher Hibbert, *The Roots of Evil* (Harmondsworth, 1966), p. 263.

111. Kingsley Davis and Wilbert E. Moore, "Some Principles of Stratification," *American Sociological Review*, 10 (April 1945), 246–47.

112. Milton Gordon, "Social Class in American Sociology," *American Journal of Sociology*, 55 (1950), 262–68.

113. Gillies, "Murder in the West of Scotland," p. 1089.

114. Wolfgang, *Patterns*, p. 331; also pp. 36–39, 142–43, 330, 334.

115. Schafer, "Criminal-Victim Relationships," pp. 55–95.

116. Ibid., pp. 93–95.

117. Ralph Banay, "Study in Murder," *Murder and the Penalty of Death, The Annals of the American Academy of Political and Social Science* (November 1952).

118. Schafer, "Criminal-Victim Relationships," pp. 99–100.

119. Ibid., pp. 103–4.

120. Wolfgang, *Patterns*, p. 137. His chapter "Alcohol and Violence" (pp. 134–67) presents a comprehensive study on the topic.

121. Gillies, "Murder in the West of Scotland," p. 1091.

122. *District of Columbia Crime Report*, p. 45.

123. Hentig, *The Criminal and His Victim*, Chapter XII, "The Contribution of the Victim to Genesis of Crime."

124. Wolfgang, *Patterns*, p. 245.

125. D. Arn. van Krevelen, "The Child as Victim," *Fourth International Criminological Congress, Papers* (The Hague, 1960), Vol. II, No. 2, p. 1.

126. Wolfgang, *Patterns*, p. 252.

127. Ibid., pp. 264–65.

128. Gillies, "Murder in the West of Scotland," p. 1088.

129. Schafer, "Criminal-Victim Relationships," pp. 107–9.

130. James V. Bennett, "Evaluating a Prison," *Annals* (May 1954), p. 10.

131. *Uniform Crime Reports*, 1965, pp. 27–29.

132. Wolfgang, *Patterns*, p. 180.

133. Gibson and Klein, "Murder," p. 43.

134. Schafer, "Criminal-Victim Relationships," p. 115.

135. Gillies, "Murder in the West of Scotland," pp. 1089–90.

136. M. de Guerry, *Essai sur la statistique morale de la France* (Paris, 1833).

137. Adolphe Quetelet, *Physique sociale, un essai sur la dévelopement des facultés de l'homme* (Paris, 1869).

138. Leone Levi, "The Seasons," *Journal of the Statistical Society*, XLIII (London, 1880), 426.

139. G. von Mayr, *Statistik und Gesellschaftslehre* (Tübingen, 1917), Vol. 3.

140. Enrico Ferri, "Variations thermométriques et criminalité," *Archives d'Anthropolgie Criminelle et des Sciences Pénales* (Lyon, 1886).

141. William Douglas Morrison, *Crime and Its Causes* (London, 1891).

142. A. Meyer, *Die Verbrechen in ihrem Zusammenhang mit dem wirtschaflichten und sozialen Verhältnissen in Kanton Zürich, Abhängigkeit von tellurischen Faktoren*, Staatswissenschaftliche Studien (Jena, 1895).

143. P. Gaedeken, "Contribution statistique a la réaction de l'organisme sous l'influence physico-chimique des agents météorologiques," *Archives d'Anthropologie Criminelle de Médecine Légale*, 24 (Lyon, 1909), 173–87.

144. See Ernst Roesner's paper "Jahreszeiten," in Alexander Elster and Heinrich Lingemann, *Handwörterbuch der Kriminologie und der anderen strafrechtlichen Hilfswissenschaften* (1st ed., Berlin, 1933), Vol. 1, pp. 688–711.

145. *Uniform Crime Reports, 1965*, pp. 6–11.

146. Wolfgang, *Patterns*, pp. 96–108.

147. Schafer, "Criminal-Victim Relationships," pp. 124–52.

148. Wolfgang, *Patterns*, pp. 120–33.

149. Gillies, "Murder in the West of Scotland," p. 1091.

150. Gibson and Klein, "Murder," pp. 30–31.

151. Wolfgang, *Patterns*, pp. 84–88.

152. *Uniform Crime Reports, 1965*, p. 106.

153. Schafer, "Criminal-Victim Relationships," pp. 206–8.

154. Wolfgang, *Patterns*, pp. 86–87.

155. Schafer, "Criminal-Victim Relationships," p. 210.

156. *The Challenge of Crime in a Free Society*, pp. 38–43; *Task Force Report: Crime and Its Impact*, pp. 80–84.

157. *Task Force Report: Crime and Its Impact*, p. 80.

158. *Crimes and Victims: A Report on the Dayton-San Jose Pilot Survey of Victimization.* LEAA (Washington, D.C., June 1974).

159. *Criminal Victimization Surveys in 13 American Cities*, LEAA (Washington, D.C., June 1975). Surveys were also conducted in Boston, Mass., Buffalo, N.Y., Cincinnati, Ohio, Houston, Texas, Miami, Fla., Milwaukee,

Wis., Minneapolis, Minn., New Orleans, La., Oakland, Calif., Pittsburgh, Pa., San Diego, Calif., and Washington, D.C.

160. *Criminal Victimization in the United States,* Vol. I, LEAA (Washington, D.C., May 1975).

161. Philip H. Ennis, *Criminal Victimization in the United States: A Report of a National Survey,* President's Commission on Law Enforcement and Administration of Justice, Field Surveys II (Washington, D.C., May 1967).

162. Ibid., pp. 1–5.

163. Beniamin Mendelsohn, "Victimology and the Needs of Contemporary Society," unpublished, Xeroxed, presented to the *First International Symposium on Victimology,* September 2–6, 1973, Jerusalem.

164. Ibid., p. 5.

165. Paul Cornil, "La notion de victimologie et sa place dans la criminologie," unpublished paper, Xeroxed, presented to the *First International Symposium on Victimology,* September 2–6, 1973, Jerusalem, p. 4.

166. Most of them, as a sort of minutes of the convention, have been published in five volumes, edited by Israel Drapkin and Emilio Viano: *Victimology, A New Focus* (Lexington, Mass., 1974–75).

167. Hugo Adam Bedou, "Are There Really Crimes Without Victims?" unpublished paper, Xeroxed, presented to the *First International Symposium on Victimology,* September 2–6, 1973, Jerusalem.

168. Milo Tyndel, "Offenders without Victims," unpublished paper, Xeroxed, presented to the *First International Symposium on Victimology,* September 2–6, 1973, Jerusalem.

169. Schneider, *Victimologie,* p. 11.

170. Edwin M. Schur, *Crimes Without Victims* (Englewood Cliffs, N.J., 1965).

171. Thomas S. Adler and Jehudit Stern, "The Psychopathology and Psychodynamics of Youth and Children in Holocaust Survivors," unpublished paper, Xeroxed, presented to the *First International Symposium on Victimology,* September 2–6, 1973, Jerusalem.

172. Louis Proal, *Political Crime* (New York, 1898).

173. Stanley W. Johnston, "Toward a Supra-national Criminology," unpublished paper, Xeroxed, presented to the *First International Symposium on Victimology,* September 2–6, 1973, Jerusalem.

174. David Shichor, "The Wrongfully Accused and the Criminal Justice System," unpublished paper, Xeroxed, presented to the *First International Symposium on Victimology,* September 2–6, 1973, Jerusalem.

175. Ann C. Burgess and Lynda Lytle Holmstrom, "Rape: the Victim and the Criminal Justice System," unpublished paper, Xeroxed, presented to the *First International Symposium on Victimology,* September 2–6, 1973, Jerusalem.

176. Steve Nelson and Menachem Amir, "The Hitch-hike Victim of Rape," unpublished paper, Xeroxed, presented to the *First International Symposium on Victimology,* September 2–6, 1973, Jerusalem.

177. Inkeri Anttila, "Victimology—a New Territory in Criminology," unpublished paper, Xeroxed, presented to the *First International Symposium on Victimology,* September 2–6, 1973, Jerusalem.

178. Ante Carich, "The Motive in Victimology," unpublished paper, Xeroxed, presented to the *First International Symposium on Victimology,* September 2–6, 1973, Jerusalem.

179. Pietro Nuvolone, "La victime dans la genése du crime," unpublished paper, Xeroxed, presented to the *First International Symposium on Victimology,* September 2–6, 1973, Jerusalem.

180. Jeffrey H. Reiman, "Victims, Harm and Justice," unpublished paper, Xeroxed, presented to the *First International Symposium on Victimology,* September 2–6, 1973, Jerusalem.

181. J.E. Mack, "A Victim-role Typology of Rational-economic Property Crime," unpublished paper, Xeroxed, presented to the *First International Symposium on Victimology,* September 2–6, 1973, Jerusalem.

3

Compensation and Restitution to Victims of Crime

Prospects of Compensation

Damages and Compensation

An important aspect of the revival of the importance of the victim is the introduction of the practice of restitution or compensation for the victim. At present there are five different systems for restitution or compensation to victims of crime.

1. Damages, civil in character and awarded in civil proceedings. In this case, the penal law is not concerned with any damage that the victim may have suffered as a result of the crime. Crime is regarded as an offense exclusively against the state; the interests of the victim play no part whatsoever in the criminal procedure. This divorcing of the victim's restitutive or compensatory claim from the penal proceedings may be regarded as an extreme manifestation of the segregation of civil and criminal wrong.

Where this segregation is in effect, the victim must seek a legal remedy for his injury through the civil courts, where the provisions of civil procedure apply. Besides India and Pakistan, and, up to recent times, New Zealand, the federal law of the United States utilizes this purely civil solution, though some state laws not only allow a claim for compensation to be entertained within the scope of the criminal procedure, but utilize the penal law in order to enforce the victim's claim.

2. Compensation, civil in character but awarded in criminal proceedings. This treatment of the problem of restitution seems to occur most frequently, but it is rarely applied in court practice. Since in this solution the clear distinction between civil and criminal wrong is still maintained, and since its administration within the framework of the criminal trial is therefore not mandatory, the courts tend to avoid applying it. Actually, in this variation a claim for restitution is allowed to be brought up as part of a criminal hearing.

In the German legal system, the hearing of such compensatory claims in criminal proceedings is termed "Adhäsionprozess," and this in itself indicates that the criminal part of the trial dominates the procedure and takes precedence over the hearing of the victim's claim; the hearing of the criminal case and that of victim compensation are, in fact, independent of each other. In France, the victim's restitutive claim is known as "l'action civile," and at the criminal trial the victim is merely a "civil partie." In Hungarian law, the damage caused to the victim by a crime, though it can be sued for during the criminal procedure, is sued for by means of a "civil claim" only. In general, all legal systems that apply this solution to the problem of compensation emphasize the civil character of the victim's claim, although allowing it to be brought up during criminal proceedings. The predominance of the criminal case is ensured by various restrictions. First of all, almost all legal systems provide that, in cases where the victim's compensatory civil claim is going to cause inconvenience, the criminal court is allowed to direct that the victim's civil claim be heard in a civil court. This restriction is based on the consideration that the court's attention should not be diverted from the criminal case by work of a civil nature; such work is not the court's proper function.

In none of the legal systems *must* the injured victim bring his claim against the wrongdoer before a criminal court, and even where the criminal court has considered the victim's claim suitable in the criminal procedure, the decision is made by means of civil procedural provisions (see for example, the systems of the Dominican Republic, France, Holland, Hungary, Israel, Norway, Sweden, and other countries).

3. Restitution, civil in character but intermingled with penal characteristics and awarded in criminal proceedings. In this solution to the problem, which is strikingly different from the solutions previously mentioned, the victim's claim must be decided by the criminal court. While even here the restitution may retain civil characteristics, there can be no doubt of its general punitive nature.

One form of this restitution is the compensatory fine, generally known as "Busse," which appears primarily in the German and Swiss legal systems, but also in some United States laws, and in the law of Mexico. Essentially it is a monetary obligation imposed upon the offender as an indemnity to the victim, and is in addition to the punishment that would be ordinarily imposed by the criminal court.

In another type of compensatory fine, the court is authorized to go over the actual damage suffered by the victim and to require the offender to pay as much as double or triple the value of the injury. This can also be found in the laws of some of the states of the United States. It is punitive to the extent that the award exceeds the actual loss. If the offender fulfills his obligation to indemnify the victim, the criminal proceedings may be closed and the offender discharged without punishment. By allowing restitution in lieu of punishment, the criminal law involves itself closely with the claim of the victim.

4. Compensation, civil in character, awarded in criminal proceedings and backed by the resources of the state. Here, as it existed in the Cuban system before Castro, compensation had no penal aspects whatsoever, and though it was awarded during criminal proceedings, it remained a purely civil institution. In this form of compensation, the state steps into the legal shoes of the offender, as it were, and undertakes to fulfill all the indemnificatory obligations imposed upon him by the court. A fund, specially set up and drawn from various sources, endeavors to perform, in the offender's stead, his compensatory obligations, and the victim is thus freed from the trouble of deciding how to enforce his claim. Having satisfied the victim's claim, the state seeks reimbursement from the offender.

It would not, perhaps, be going too far to say that this not only shows concern on the part of the state for the victim's interests, but may imply a recognition by the state that it has failed in its duty to protect the victim and to prevent the commission of the crime.

5. Compensation, neutral in character and awarded through a special procedure. This system is in force in Switzerland (since 1937), in New Zealand (since 1963), in the United Kingdom (since 1964), in some states of the United States, and in the United States federal proposals. It applies in cases in which the victim is in need and in which the offender appears to be insolvent and unable to satisfy the victim's claim for damages. Neither the civil nor the criminal courts are competent to exercise jurisdiction, but a separate and independent procedure leads to intervention by the state on the application of the victim. If the victim is successful in his application, the state compensates him for the injury or damage caused by the crime.

Since the injured person appears neither as victim nor as plaintiff, but merely as an applicant, neither the procedure nor the indemnification can be termed either civil or criminal. It can even be argued as to whether this is restitution or compensation performed by the state or merely state assistance to a person whose loss or need was caused by a criminal offense.[1] It may resemble the California system and, in general, the trend toward compensation laws that is beginning in America.

The persistent apathy toward compensation for the victim as an issue in criminal procedure may be one of the fundamental obstacles to providing higher legal status to the criminal-victim relationship. This apathy has prevented acceptance of the restitution concept except in its narrowest form. With almost no exception, restitution or compensation (not to be confused with advocating the satisfaction of the victim's vital needs) to victims of crime is restricted to payment of civil damages, and its inclusion in criminal law would be regarded an achievement. In the penal systems mentioned above, the place of restitution in criminal law is evidenced by a legal situation in which criminal law merely provides a formalistic recording of a civil law performance. Although this obviously leads to reparation, it can result only in a virtual criminological mummification of civil law provisions. However, even this static and minimal understanding runs into difficulties, and the victim of crime continues to be ignored.

Nevertheless, the idea of compensation to victims of crime, an idea reborn in the middle of the twentieth century along with the idea of the importance of the victim's role, attracted particular interest by the late 1950s and is today being developed, however tediously, into an operationally administrative reality. The late Margery Fry was probably the first to urge acceptance of the idea and her pen drew popular attention to the case of a man in England who was blinded as the consequence of a criminal offense and was therefore awarded compensation of £11,500. Considering the fact that his two assailants were ordered to pay him five shillings weekly, "the victim will need to live another 442 years to collect the last installment." Thus Margery Fry commented on the effectiveness of England's present-day compensation system.[2] Her plea for "better help" for the victim of crime is, like so many other modern ideas in criminal law and criminology, not a new notion at all. However, when the idea was raised, under the impressive title of "justice for victims," it had a very favorable reception and on several occasions was discussed in the House of Commons.

This revival of the idea of victim compensation prompted the American "Round Table" articles.[3] In these articles several persons gave practical criticism of the English proposal, and objected to the principle of state compensation and the abandonment of individual responsibility. Among other things, concern was expressed for "the sociological decadence that could come from that kind of thinking." However, practical benefits were also mentioned, and "the greater interest on the part of the public in the matter of law enforcement if the state compensation were to be adopted" was pointed out.[4] One commentator suggested that "the insured victim hardly fits the picture of the unfortunate object of pity. . . . he simply calls up his insurance company and lets them worry about it."[5] It was also argued that to restrict compensation to violent crime, as the late Margery Fry suggested, is to make an arbitrary and unnecessary distinction.[6]

In England, the Home Secretary's White Paper on "Penal Practice in a Changing Society," presented to the Parliament in February 1959, drew attention to the fact that "the assumption that the claims of the victim are sufficiently satisfied if the offender is punished by society becomes less persuasive" and "suggests . . . a reconsideration of the position of the victims of crime." Also reported in this White Paper was a commission given to Stephen Schafer by the British Home Office, to work on the problem of restitution: this was the first such study in modern times.[7]

Later on, a Private Member's Bill, "The Criminal Injuries (Compensation) Bill" was presented to the House of Commons. Submitted by R.E. Prentice, it attempted to solve the restitution problem from the angle of insurance.[8]

Later another White Paper[9] was presented to Parliament, and then a third,[10] this time jointly with the Scottish Home Office. Both were entitled "Compensation for Victims of Crimes of Violence." Debates were held on May 4, 1964, in the House of Commons; on May 7, 1964, in the House of Lords; and on June 24, 1964, in the House of Commons. On August 1, 1964, the British government introduced a nonstatutory scheme on an experimental basis and appointed a "Criminal Injuries Compensation Board" to administer it. Through this Board compensation is assessed on the basis of common law damages and takes the form of a lump-sum payment.[11]

Italy is also preparing a victim-compensation scheme.[12]

New Zealand, somewhat before the English experiment, passed "An Act to provide for the compensation of persons injured by certain criminal acts, and of dependents of persons killed by such acts."[13] This became effective on January 1, 1964. In this case, too, an appointed "Crimes Compensation Tribunal" is in charge of awarding a nonstatutory payment of compensation. In his evaluative description of this scheme, Bruce J. Cameron suggests that the New Zealand act has two advantages: "There is the material benefit from the awards of compensation that may be made by the tribunal, and in addition there is the psychological effect on the community produced by the very fact that there is such a scheme in existence."[14] It is worth mentioning that the New Zealand government is now considering an extension and modification of its legislation in order to provide compensation for those who sustain a property loss through the acts of escaped prisoners during the course of escape.[15]

Restitution and Compensation

Restitution and *compensation,* terms often used interchangeably, represent in fact two different points of view. Compensation, in criminal-victim relationships, concerns the counterbalancing of the victim's loss that results from the criminal attack. It means making amends to him; or, perhaps better stated, it is compensation for the damage or injury caused by a crime against him. It is an indication of the responsibility of the society; it is a claim for compensating action by the society; it is civil in character and thus represents a noncriminal goal in a criminal case. As opposed to compensation, restitution in criminal-victim relationships concerns reparation of the victim's loss or, better, restoration of his position and rights that were damaged or destroyed by and during the criminal attack. It is an indication of the responsibility of the offender; it is a claim for restitutive action on the part of the offender; it is penal in character and thus represents a correctional goal in a criminal case. Compensation calls for action by the victim in the form of an application, and payment by society; restitution calls for a decision by a criminal court and payment by the offender.

The purpose of this book is not to give an account of the centuries-old dispute about the difference between criminal and civil wrongs; still less is it intended to argue this much disputed question, which is one of those problems of the legal sciences in which a spectacular multiplicity of opinions have for so long differed. "Compensation versus restitution" is concerned with the problem of the extent to which legal systems try to separate criminal and civil wrongs, both theoretically and practically. At present, the majority of legal provisions call for compensation based on the principle of distinguishing between criminal and civil wrong. Such systems reject the unitary view of wrong, which sees wrong as simply a breach of the law, it being immaterial what sort of law is transgressed. The present general view and the American trend is toward compensation: no matter what the cause of the loss or the injury may be, the claim (for compensation), even if it was caused by crime, is considered a civil matter only and is not to be connected with the disposition of the criminal case and correctional action against the criminal. The American experiments with so-called "victim-advocacies" and "mediation committees," working with some courts, seem to mix the criminal and civil aspects, moreover, they appear to make a civil case of a criminal offense.

However, a thoughtful consideration of the place of compensation or restitution in our norm-system calls for more than speculation about the elusive boundary between criminal and civil wrongs. It would be well to begin by abandoning traditional concepts of what is and what is not the state's interest in the suppression of crime. In spite of theoretical distinctions, criminal law and civil law seem to be more integrated than ever before. It was not inappropriate for ancient Roman jurists to describe punishment as "satisfaction." Indeed, the victim not only tends to think of criminal justice as nationalized vengeance, but also expects indemnification for the damage caused him. The victim expects the criminal to be morally reproached for the crime; in addition he expects a certain degree of injury to be inflicted upon the offender in order to satisfy his desire for revenge.

If it were realized that this "spiritual" satisfaction is implicit in any system of punishment, a new concept of the purpose of punishment might arise. In addition to protection of law and order in the abstract and reform of the criminal, the victim's claim to restitution can be a third element of punishment. In the retributive sense, restitution exists in punishment even at present, but true restitution can develop only if spiritual satisfaction is replaced by material satisfaction.

When Kathleen Smith recommended the "self-determinate prison sentence" as "a cure for crime," and proposed that all victims of crime should be "compensated" through the personal labor of the prisoner in the correctional institution, she was illustrating the idea of restitution made personally by the offender.[16] This proposal has been expressed by many others during the past 70 years. As early as some 450 years ago, Sir Thomas More, in *Utopia,* proposed restitution ("to the right owner, and not, as they do in other lands, to the king") so that the offenders themselves should be "condemned to be common laborers, and, unless the theft is very heinous, they are neither locked in prison, nor kept in fetters, but are untied and go at large, laboring on the public works." In connection with the punitive aspects of restitution, Herbert Spencer suggested that restitution should be made through prison work and the prisoner's income and that the offender should be kept in prison until restitution is completed.[17] Another suggestion was made by Garofalo. He felt that in cases where the offender is solvent, his property should be confiscated and restitution made therefrom by order of the court; if insolvent, he should be made to work for the state.[18] Still another proposal, made by Prins and also by Garofalo, was to balance the burden of fines and restitution between the rich and the poor. According to this proposal, a poor man would pay in days of work, a rich man by income or salary based on an equal number of days of work. If, say $2 represented the value of a day's work, and the poor man were sentenced to pay $2, he would be released after giving one day's labor to the victim. The rich man, instead of being sentenced to so many days of labor, would pay out of income or salary an amount based on an equal number of days of work. If this represented, say $200 a day, he would have to pay accordingly.[19]

The "noble way" to care for the victim is to make it possible for the offender to fulfill his obligation through income from work.[20] This noble way may be very effective, provided that it is not forgotten that the corrective-punitive side of restitution can be a valuable aid to reforming the criminal. Schafer proposed "correctional restitution" and suggested that if the offender were at liberty after punishment, but had to make restitution through work, restitution would retain its punitive-reformative character. At the same time, the state would be relieved to a certain extent of the need to solve the problem of restitution; however, the criminal court should have to consider this question within the scope of the criminal procedure that deals with the criminal case itself.[21] As Albert Eglash suggested, restitution should be made by the offender; it ought not to be something done for him or to him. And since it requires effort on his part, it may be especially useful in strengthening his feelings of responsibility.[22] If performance of the restitutive obligation affects the freedom of work of the offender, or even his personal liberty, this would constitute an extension of his punishment. If restitution is unconnected with the criminal procedure involving the actual offense and is performed by the state for the criminal, this would be compensation that is civil in character and not far removed from the concept of damages.

Thus, if the criminal-victim relationship is to be maintained to the very end of the criminal case, punitive restitution—not damages, and not even restitutive punishment—seems to be the effective way of developing and utilizing the functional responsibility of the participants in the crime.

Compensation in Other Countries

It may be useful to show how compensation systems in other countries operate. Switzerland, New Zealand, and the United Kingdom (England, Wales, and Scotland) may call for special attention since they have indemnification systems that are probably typical of present-day trends. They are, of course, only examples here: many other countries also have compensation systems.

Victim Compensation in Switzerland

In investigating the Swiss system, one has to face the difficulty that Swiss law involves the provisions of twenty-six bodies of cantonal law in addition to the legislation of the Swiss Federation itself.[23] They have similar but not identical provisions. Even the terms used for the claimant differ: *private complainment, civil plaintiff, interested party, informer,* and *injured party* are only a few of the many cantonal terms. This alone suggests that, though restitution has some relation to both criminal law and to what may be called "neutral" procedure, generally it leans toward being civil in character.

The victim must first of all choose between participating in the criminal procedure or making an independent claim in a civil-type court. If he claims compensation in the criminal court, this is dealt with by the so-called *adhesive procedure.* This is similar to the provisions of German law and also has a limited chance of success; in other words, the claim will succeed only if it does not hold up the exclusively criminal proceedings.

If, however, the victim forgoes his claim for restitution, with the result that the trial proceeds smoothly, he may obtain damages as follows:

1. The victim of a criminal injury, for which the offender will not make compensation, may be awarded the proceeds—to the extent of his claim as established by court decision or by agreement —from the sale of confiscated objects, gifts, or other things that go to the state. In addition, he may be awarded a sum that the state has demanded from the offender as a guarantee that he will keep the peace.

2. In the case of a person who has suffered severe hardship as the result of a criminal injury, for which compensation is not forthcoming, an award may be made from the *Busse* paid by the convicted person. This seems to involve a procedure independent of either the civil courts or the criminal court that hears the case. However, the state is under no obligation to make this kind of award, and in practice the procedure is rare.

The victim has little chance of enforcing his claim against the prisoner's earnings and usually can turn only to civil proceedings. Prisoners are allowed to offer a part of their prison earnings toward compensating the victim (some cantons seem to envisage this in their legislation), but their earnings, the so-called *peculium,* are far less than those of free workers and have no real significance as far as restitution is concerned.[24]

Revision of Switzerland's penal laws is at hand and in fact has been partly realized, but there are no signs that the rules that deal with restitution or compensation to victims of crime are likely to be altered.[25]

Victim Compensation in New Zealand

"The South Pacific country of New Zealand has, since the end of the nineteenth century, enjoyed a reputation for advanced legislation in social matters."[26] One of the examples of this distinctive legislative trend is the New Zealand Act "to provide for the compensation of persons injured by certain criminal acts, and of dependents of persons killed by such Acts."[27] The short title of the act is "Criminal Injuries Compensation Act 1963." This act came into force on January 1, 1964, shortly before England's pioneering efforts materialized. The philosophy behind this New Zealand law was "rather the community's duty towards those who suffer misfortune than the liability of the state for failing to prevent crime."[28]

To implement this act, a "Crimes Compensation Tribunal," consisting of three members, was set up and was appointed for a term of five years by the Governor General (on the recommendation of the Minister of Justice). The chairman of the tribunal must be a lawyer of the supreme court with not less than seven years' practice. This tribunal is a "Commission of Inquiry." The chairman is given the power to issue summonses requiring witnesses to appear before the tribunal or requiring the production of documents, or to do any other act preliminary to or incidental to the hearing of any matter of compensation. When an application is made, the tribunal fixes a time and place for the hearing, receives the evidence, and concludes the hearing with an "order." There is no appeal against any decision by the tribunal.

The tribunal has power to award compensation in cases in which a person is injured or killed by any of the following criminal acts:

- completed or attempted rape
- sexual intercourse or indecency with a girl under 12
- indecent assault on a girl between 12 and 16, or on a woman, or on a boy, or on a man
- completed or attempted murder or manslaughter
- wounding with intent
- injuring with intent or by unlawful act
- aggravated assault, wounding, or injury
- assault with intent to injure
- assault on a child or by a male on a female
- common assault
- disabling
- discharging a firearm or doing a dangerous act with intent
- acid throwing
- poisoning with intent
- infecting with disease
- endangering transport
- abduction of a woman or a girl
- kidnapping

In determining whether to order compensation for a victim or his dependents, the tribunal concerns itself with all matters that it considers relevant in any particular case: matters such as age, insanity, drunkenness, or legal incapability in the case of the offender. As to the victim, it concerns itself with any behavior that directly or indirectly contributed to his injury or death. In doing all this, the New Zealand legislation opened the way to the legal consideration of victim-precipitated crimes.

Compensation can be awarded for expenses, pecuniary loss, and also for the pain and suffering of the victim. The amount of compensation is left entirely to the discretion of the tribunal. It may be a lump sum or may consist of periodic payments.

No compensation can be made for loss or damage to property; the orders of the tribunal are restricted to personal injuries. According to this New Zealand law "injury" means actual bodily harm, pregnancy, and mental or nervous shock.[29]

Applications for compensation during the first two years of the law have been surprisingly few. In the first year seven awards were made; in the second, nine awards.[30]

In many cases the question of provocation had to be considered; this often required examination of police and court documents.[31]

The New Zealand act provides for recovery from the offender of amounts paid to the victim. In effect, the state compensates the latter and endeavors to collect from the former, taking into account his income and family responsibilities.[32]

As the Ministry of Justice of New Zealand reported, the act has not been used as much as had been expected. Its cost to the taxpayer has therefore been small. No unexpected difficulties have been encountered in the operation of the law, and the government is considering the extension of the compensation scheme, first of all to cases in which escaped prisoners cause harm or injury.[33]

Victim Compensation in England

The idea of restitution to victims of crime is not new, but "the idea that the victims of crimes should be compensated by State action is comparatively recent."[34] Although Cuba and Switzerland have had such a scheme for many years, and although New Zealand introduced one before England, England (and Wales and Scotland) will no doubt be remembered as the pioneer of present-day victim compensation. After a decade of arduous struggle for public recognition, England's compensation scheme has developed "not because the State is under a legal liability to pay," but because—as some sort of social obligation or perhaps as a part of social policy and an extension of the welfare system—it was felt "that provision should be made for victims of crimes of violence."[35]

The scheme is based on two fundamental points. The first point is that claims for compensation should be determined by a judicial or quasi-judicial body. The second point is that they should be payable only in deserving cases; in other words, the victim of a crime of violence should not be entitled automatically to compensation. The latter point refers to victim-guilt or victim-precipitated crimes. It takes into account whether "the victim himself was partly to blame."[36] The British government has "decided on a scheme based on common law damages rather than on the Industrial Injuries Scheme."[37]

The scheme "represents a hesitant step in the right direction."[38] This is why only *ex gratia* payments are designed, and it has been considered "best to start with a flexible scheme which can be altered in the light of experience,"[39] in other words, in an experimental and nonstatutory form. Nevertheless, "while no one suggested that the State 'was' responsible for the victim's misfortune, it was generally agreed, that the State 'should' accept responsibility."[40] Indeed, "if society, by its indifference to those things which inculcate proper behavior, continues to make its contribution to the breeding of criminals, it must accept a large measure of responsibility for the consequences of criminal acts."[41]

The compensation scheme is administered by a body known as the Criminal Injuries Compensation Board, which is appointed by the Home Secretary (in Scotland by the Secretary of State for Scotland) after consultation with the Lord Chancellor. The chairman of the board must necessarily be a person of wide legal experience, and the other members are also legally qualified. The board is completely responsible for deciding how much compensation should be paid in individual cases, and its decisions are not subject to appeal or ministerial review.

The board entertains applications for *ex gratia* payments of compensation in cases where personal injury is directly attributable to:

1. a criminal offense;
2. an arrest or an attempted arrest of an offender or a suspected offender;
3. the prevention or attempted prevention of an offense;
4. helping any constable who is engaged in arresting or attempting to arrest an offender or suspected offender, or who is engaged in preventing or attempting to prevent an offense.

If the injury causes at least three weeks' loss of earnings, or if it is an injury for which not less than £50 (about $140) compensation would be awarded, the circumstances of the injury are reported to the police without delay or become the subject of criminal court proceedings, and the applicant submits himself to a medical examination.

In cases of rape or sexual assaults, the board considers applications for compensation with respect to pain, suffering, and shock, and also with respect to loss of earnings due to pregnancy resulting from rape. But compensation is not payable for the maintenance of any child born as a result of a sexual offense. Also, offenses committed against a member of the offender's family who is living with him are excluded from compensation, as are motoring offenses (except where the motor vehicle has been used as a weapon).

The board considers whether, because of provocation or otherwise, the victim has any share in the responsibility for the crime. In accordance with its assessment of the degree of responsibility, the board will reduce the amount of compensation or reject the claim altogether.

The scheme excludes "double compensation." The criminally injured person is not permitted to have both the compensation awarded by the board and anything obtained through an ordinary common law claim.[42]

No traditional type of appeal is open to the applicant. However, the scheme provides for a special review of cases. This review can be initiated by the applicant or by a board member. In accordance with the normal procedural custom of the board, the initial decision is made by one of its members, who communicates his conclusions to the applicant. If the applicant is not satisfied with this decision, he is entitled to a hearing before three other members of the board (Appellate Tribunal). The member who made the initial decision is not one of them.

When a board member feels that he cannot reach a "just and proper" decision, he too can refer the application to the Appellate Tribunal.[43]

The Criminal Injuries Compensation Board, after being in existence for only eight months as of March 31, 1965, released its first interim report without commenting on or analyzing the cases.[44] Another report, released in January 1966, summarized some of the cases disposed of by the end of 1965.[45] It also gave an account of 2,216 applications submitted to the board from its inception to December 31, 1965, and an account of £304,643 (about $853,-000) awarded during this seventeen-month period. By the end of 1965, however, out of 2,216 cases, only 1,184 cases were closed, and 1,032 applicants were still waiting for a decision. A majority of the cases were settled by a single member of the board; only 32 cases went to hearings, and in only 19 did the applicant ask for a hearing because he disagreed with a one-member decision.

A summary of selected cases includes the following:

- A woman, 59, was seriously assaulted in a dark passageway and had to be hospitalized for two months. She received a compensation of £582 (about $1,630).

- A woman, 33, was attacked with a knife by her husband, from whom she was separated, and was unable to work for four months. She was awarded £500 (about $1,400).

- A girl, 14, was struck with a chopper by a boy, 12, after an argument. She received £255 (about $714).

- A woman, 67, attacked by a stranger and sexually assaulted, suffered severe shock. It seemed unlikely that she would ever be able to work again. She was awarded £2,020 (about $5,565).

- A girl, 7, indecently assaulted, received £251 (about $702).

- A male bus conductor, 26, assaulted by youths who refused to pay their fares, was unable to work for ten weeks. He received £368 (about $1,030).

- A man, 29, a storehouse caretaker, caught thieves in the act. The thieves deliberately drove a van into him and struck him down while he was trying to prevent their escape. He was awarded £225 (about $630).

- A boy, 7, was hit in the eye by an airgun pellet fired by one of three boys, aged 13 to 15. He suffered permanent eye damage. His compensation was £2,250 (about $6,300).

- Another boy, 17, was kicked and stabbed by a gang of youths. He suffered a permanently weakened grip of the right hand and an impaired function of the other hand. He received £773 (about $2,164).

- A man, 60, was punched and knocked down by a stranger. He was taken to a hospital and was dead on arrival. His skull had been fractured. His widow, 60, was granted a retirement pension of £4.0.6d (about $12) a week.

In some other cases the awards were reduced or no compensation was awarded. A reduction by 50 percent of the compensation applied for was decided in a case in which the victim, under the influence of alcohol, provoked the person who struck him. In another case, where the victim was shot in the face during a dispute over shooting rights on farmland, his responsibility was assessed at 10 percent. No award was given to a man, 57, who was cut by glass from a shop window that had been broken by a young man during a struggle to hold a suspect until the police arrived (the suspect was charged). The board was not satisfied that the injury was directly attributable to a criminal offense. No award was granted to a man, 24, who was stabbed by his mother-in-law, with whom he and his wife shared an apartment. The application was denied because an offense had been committed against a member of the assailant's family while all were living together. In another case, the Appellate Tribunal dismissed the application because the circumstances of the injury had not been reported to the police as required by the rules.[46]

The number of applications and of awarded compensatory payments is much higher in England, Scotland, and Wales than in New Zealand. Only further research and further comparative analysis of crime rates and other factors, together with future developments, can explain this disparity.

Victim Compensation in Australia

The Australian system, operating in New South Wales and in Queensland, is different from that of New Zealand, both in form and philosophy.[47] The New South Wales law, the first in Australia, refers back to their Crime Act of 1900, which provides that if a person is convicted of any felony or misdemeanor, the court, at the time of conviction or thereafter, can direct a certain sum to be paid out of the property of the offender. According to the New South Wales Criminal Injuries Compensation Act of 1967, however, where the court makes a compensation order for an injury—specifically defined as bodily harm, but including pregnancy, and mental and nervous shock—the victim (called the "aggrieved person") may apply to the State Treasury for payments to him from the Consolidated Revenue Fund. The victim can apply even if the offender was acquitted in case if the court orders the payment in spite of the acquittal. However, compensation to the victim of crime by the State Treasury is not a right of the victim, but is a payment by grace (*ex gratia*) of the state; thus, the victim is simply eligible to apply for compensation, and the State Treasury decides whether or not the court order entitles the victim to compensation from the offender or by the state.

The Queensland scheme is similar to that of New South Wales. Here the 1968 law provides the same procedure, except that not the State Treasury, but the government decides the *ex gratia* payment. In 1969 South Australia introduced a victim compensation legislation, with hardly any difference from the Queensland system. In 1970 Western Australia copied the New South Wales model. Based on the New South Wales and Queensland legislation, a Criminal Injuries Compensation Act was attempted in 1971 by the Tasmanian Parliament, but it failed to pass.

Unique to Australia is the statute that was enacted in Victoria in 1972. It is modelled after the New Zealand system, but it goes further. The Victorian Crime Compensation Tribunal may compensate victims of *any* crime—crimes are not named or listed (it can be assault, robbery, theft, or anything else)—and the only restriction is that the criminal offense should be punishable by imprisonment. This law, however, like all other compensation laws in Australia, recognizes the criminal-victim relationship and the responsibility of the victim by restricting compensation in cases where the victim is a relative of the offender or a member of his household, and in cases where the victim directly or indirectly contributed to the crime.

Victim Compensation in Finland

The Finnish law for compensating victims of crime from public funds was passed in the Parliament in late 1973 and came into force by March 1, 1974.[48] The law stands out from other victim compensation systems by offering damages caused not only to persons, but also to property. Nevertheless, the latter case is restricted to victims of those offenders who for vagabondage, abuse of intoxicants, mental illness, retardedness, drunkenness, or the like have been institutionalized or otherwise deprived of their freedom, while in an institution or on vacation from or having escaped from an institution or are under the custody of the law, or to victims of children or young persons who, under the Law for the Protection of Children, have been taken into custody.[49] Traffic-connected injuries are compensated through the Traffic Insurance Act of 1959. As in Victoria, Australia, Finland's victim compensation law also takes into account the criminal-victim relationships and the responsibility of the victim: should the offender and the victim live in the same household, compensation to the victim of crime is granted only in exceptional circumstances, and if the victim proved to be instrumental in the development of crime, the compensation is to be adjusted accordingly. Basically, the State Accident Office is in charge of granting the compensation, but actually a Board decides over the applications.

By the end of the first year of operation, close to 300 applications were submitted for compensation, and approximately half of them were decided during the same period. Approximately 50 percent of the applications dealt with crimes against the person, about 21 percent with property crimes, and the rest with offenses where both personal injuries and property damages were involved. Most of the applicants were males, with the median age of 32, the majority of whom were skilled and unskilled workers.

Recommendations of International Conferences on Victim Compensation

The *First International Symposium on Victimology,* in 1973 in Jerusalem, dealt extensively with the question of compensating victims of crime. In its Conclusions and Recommendations, the Symposium recommended that all nations should, "as a matter of urgency," give consideration to the establishment of a state system of compensating victims of crime, and that the nations should seek to achieve maximum efficacy in the application of these schemes. It was also recommended that information about the operation of such systems should be widely disseminated not only to experts, but to the general public. It was further recommended that all compensation schemes be evaluated with a view to improving their application.

Among those aspects that require further examination are whether or not a maximum limit should be set on compensation awards; what kind of losses should be compensated; how should the victim precipitation be evaluated; should the state be entitled to claim reinbursement from the offender; what compensation (if any) should be awarded if the accused person was found not guilty; to what compensation should the bystander be entitled in the case of his aiding the victim; and should an office of "victim-Ombudsman" be set up (John Dussich's proposal) to provide direct assistance to the victim in order to mitigate the victim's immediate trauma, and to offer treatment to "victim-recidivists."

To prepare the Eleventh International Congress on Penal Laws in 1974, a *Preparatory Colloquium of this World Congress* was held on "compensation of victims of crime," in 1973 in the Max-Planck-Institute in Freiburg, Germany, chaired by Hans-Heinrich Jescheck. The national rapporteurs were: for the German Democratic Republic, Horst Luther and Hans Weber; for the German Federal Republic (Western Germany), Clemens Amelunxen and Johann-Georg Schätzler; for Belgium, René Jeurissen; for Brazil, Armida Bergamini Miotto; for Canada, Peter Burns and Allen M. Ross; for Egypt, Mahmoud Mostafa; for the United States of America, Stephen Schafer; for Finland, Inkeri Anttila; for Hungary, Teréz Nagy and Ervin Cséka; for Italy, Mario Pisani and Luigi Autru Ryolo; for Japan, Ryuichi Hirano; for the Netherlands, J.J.R. Bakker; for Poland, Marian Cieslak and Andrzej Murzynowski; for Roumania, Siegfried Kahane and Adrian Dimitriu; for Tanzania, David Williams; for Czechoslovakia, Antonin Ruzek and Eugen Husar; and for Yugoslavia, Alenka Selih and Peter Kobe. The Rapporteur General was the Dutch representative, Jacob M. van Bemmelen. Each national Rapporteur offered information about the system in force in his own country.[50]

The Resolutions of the Preparatory Colloquium indicated that the majority of the colloquium's participants supported the view that, subject to certain limitations, the state or other public institutions should be primarily responsible for compensating the victim of crime from public funds. The Resolutions suggested that the decision as to whether such a compensation program might be administered by an independent fund, a special compensation board, through pre-existing social welfare or social insurance agencies should be left to the various legislators. A group of the participants who favored public compensation by the state or other public institutions recommended, however, that this kind of compensation should have only a subsidiary role and leave the primary responsibility with the offender. Some other participants did not favor the creation of public compensation arrangements, believing either that the existing institutions are adequate, or that public compensation may fail.

The supporters of primary or subsidiary public compensation recommended the consideration of a number of principles in constructing a compensation system, among them that compensation should be restricted to damages resulting from intentional crimes against limb and life; that crimes by negligence and property crimes should be excluded; that compensation should be a legal right of the victim (as opposed to the *ex gratia* satisfaction); and that in the course of compensation, due regard should be paid both to the resocialization of the criminal and to the protection of the economically weak offender. It was recommended that the decision as to whether it is appropriate to structure the compensation procedure as a judicial or an administrative proceeding has to be left to the consideration of the national legislator; the criminal court should, however, be empowered to make a recommendation about the appropriateness of public compensation in its adjudication over the criminal act itself.

The Resolutions claimed that there are several advantages in the type of procedure in which the criminal responsibility of the accused person and the compensatory demand of the victim are resolved in a unitary proceeding. However, since there are also considerable drawbacks in such a procedure, no recommendation was made regarding its adoption. Some important points to be considered in structuring such a unitary procedure are that the victim must have the right to choose an ordinary civil proceeding in preference to litigating his civil claim in the criminal proceedings; that such a unitary procedure must be a mixed structure of civil and criminal procedural elements; that the victim should have the right to appeal; and that it is not the duty of the accused person to disclose his financial resources. There is still a controversy over whether the criminal court should be allowed to award compensation to the victim on its own motion, regardless of whether the victim or his agent have claimed it, or whether the criminal court has the right to decide the justification of the civil claim of the victim by leaving the decision as to the amount to a separate civil procedure.

The Resolutions covered the question of providing victim compensation through other means, that is, through indirect devices. They suggested that compensation may be imposed as a condition of nonprosecution, of probation, or of conditional release. Furthermore, and this expresses the importance of the criminal-victim relationship, it has been recommended that compensation that has been achieved or aimed at by the offender can be considered in sentencing and commutation proceedings. Although it is a part of the Resolutions that as a direct form of compensation the criminal court may require the criminal to compensate the victim either as the only or as an additional sanction of condemnation, it should be noted that several participants of this Preparatory Colloquium expressly opposed the use of victim compensation as the only sanction.

The *Eleventh International Congress of Penal Law* in 1974 in Budapest, Hungary, organized by de Association Internationale de Droit Pénal (International Association of Penal Law), essentially maintained the resolutions of the Preparatory Colloquium.

The *Second International Symposium on Victimology,* held in 1976 in Boston, Massachusetts, in its Section III on "The Victim and the Society," again discussed the problems of compensation to victims of crime, yet it had to leave the answer to several theoretical and practical questions to the following international conventions.

Victim Compensation in America

The Meetings of the American Society of Criminology

The American Society of Criminology devoted a full meeting to the problem of victim compensation. At this meeting Gerhard Mueller and John Edwards made general recommendations; Robert Childres viewed the question from the angle of personal injury; and James Starrs suggested that compensation for victims of crime be considered as part of the general problem of insurance law.

Marvin Wolfgang supported the principle that society has a responsibility to compensate the victim of a criminal assault. He suggested that this principle is neither new nor a radical departure from prevailing political and legal norms in Western culture, although legislation providing for victim compensation by the state would be an innovation in contemporary criminal law. However, Wolfgang proposed that if state compensation to the victim is adopted as a logical extension of the concern of criminal law for both parties in a two-person crime of personal violence, then some system for measuring harm is required, and some standard of, and system for, judging the degree of harm must be established. His research with Thorsten Sellin on the measurement of delinquency was offered toward this end; it reduced crimes against the person and against property to a unidimensional base, thus providing a way to equate the seriousness of the offenses. "If there is a virtue in establishing a state system of victim compensation, there should

be a virtue in exploring the dimensions of the relationship between
money values and physical harm beyond the arbitrary notions of a
legislative committee."[52]

Schafer, however, supported the idea that compensation to the
victim of crime should be the personal responsibility of the offender
and a part of the correctional process. In terms of correctional
restitution to victims of crime, the offender should understand that
he has hurt not only the state, and law and order, but also the
victim. In fact, it is the victim, primarily, who is injured, and the
abstract values of society are injured as a result. From this viewpoint, restitution not only makes good the injury or loss, but at the
same time helps in the correction, reform, and rehabilitation of
the offender, and can be regarded not as an extension but as a part
of the sentence. Correctional restitution could be a part of the
synthetic punishment, a response of criminal justice to the functional responsibility of the criminal.

The efforts of the American Society of Criminology in renewing
the interest in victim compensation were not fruitless. Law journals
and popular magazines started to publish articles on the subject.
This almost forgotten problem of restitution to victims of crime
"made its appearance on the postmidnight radio talkathons, in the
popular magazines, and the Sunday supplements. The very question—why not pay the victim of crime?—seems appealing to anyone with a social conscience."[53] Perhaps the most important recent
contribution to the victim compensation problem has been the
Minnesota Law Review Symposium.

The Minnesota Law Review Symposium and Other Professional Contributions

"An examination of the scope of the problem" was published by
the *Minnesota Law Review* in the form of a symposium on the
subject of compensation to victims of crimes of personal violence.
Contributors were Gerhard O.W. Mueller, Marvin E. Wolfgang,
Stephen Schafer, Ralph W. Yarborough, Robert D. Childres and
James E. Starrs. The editorial introduction stated that "it is hoped
that the suggestions offered, the problem posed, and the guidelines
presented will add impetus to further study and eventual solution
of this topical issue."[54]

In his article, Mueller states that the primary purpose of the symposium is "to circumscribe the grand outlines of the problem in an attempt to direct subsequent research and ultimate sociopolitical action." He attempts to clarify the concept of victim compensation and seems to accept the term "in the sense of payments by a government agency to persons injured by a criminal agency." He wonders how much this would cost and suggests that "if the Government wants to parallel the operations of a private insurance enterprise," the total cost of the administration of criminal justice should be taken into account, but that the difficulty here is that we do not know this figure. Mueller is aware of the enormous difficulties that stand in the way of victim compensation schemes, but hopes for an advance "from research thought to research action, and ultimately, to implementation."[55]

Wolfgang explores and supports the principle that society has a responsibility to compensate the victims of violent crimes. He suggests that "the federal and various state workmen's compensation laws provide a useful analogy and contemporary precedent for the proposal of victim compensation."

He also proposes "some system for measuring harm,"[56] and recommends his "measurement of delinquency," which he developed with Thorsten Sellin.[57] This offers suggestions for measuring the gravity of injury in terms of money values. Wolfgang views the victim as a contributing and supporting member of a society "which has failed to protect him against certain types of crime"; this is why the society should "undertake the obligation to compensate the victim of a criminal assault."[58]

Schafer couples his concern for the victim with an examination of the restitutive effect a compensation system can have on the offender. He proposes that the criminal be considered a member of his cultural group, and that his crime be viewed in terms of his social relationships. He suggests that attention be directed to what he tentatively calls the criminal's functional responsibility, rather than to the isolated criminal act. He recommends a scheme wherein the administrator of criminal justice would deal not with civil damages, but with "correctional restitution." This should become a part of the sentence and thus an institution of the criminal law. In terms of correctional benefits, a modern restitution system should make the offender understand that he has directly injured the victim as well as the state, and law and order. Schafer refers to his research on violent crimes: many offenders evidenced no guilt feelings and could neither understand nor accept their functional responsibility to society or to their victims. "Their understanding of incarceration seemed limited to what they viewed as merely a formal or normative wrong, which had to be paid for to the agencies of criminal justice, but to nobody else."[59]

Senator Ralph Yarborough discusses his bill to provide victim compensation within federal jurisdiction. He suggests that "the idea is so simple and just that its novelty makes less of a first impression than the regret that the idea has not been previously adopted." He views the victims as a needy class and recognizes the compensative duty of the state. Yarborough thinks that "in view of the many social welfare programs that are in operation, the failure to recognize the special claims of this group seems to be a gross oversight."[60]

Robert Childres comments upon the Yarborough bill and the California legislation. He also brings up a number of general problems, and argues with Mueller's and Schafer's approach to the restitution problem. He finds "unfortunate omissions" in the Yarborough proposal and suggests that the California welfare department will not be able to mold its statute into a decent program.

Childres calls attention to the cost of compensation and does not think it too great. He also discusses federal-state relationships, and suggests that the proposed reform will not "provoke fears of bureaucratic monsters."[61] However, fraudulent claims should be watched, although this seems to be only a marginal problem.

James Starrs discusses the problem from the angle of private insurance programs that may provide the necessary protection to victims. He has little doubt about the necessity of state compensation programs. However, "undoubtedly, more can be done and would be if insurance companies assumed a greater share of the cost of crime."

Starrs suggests that all compensation schemes have the drawback of keeping the level of payments so low that "full compensation for all damages must be a rarity under them." In his view "insurance provides the ideal setting for achieving payments more commensurate with the losses actually sustained by crime victims." In his thinking, "private insurance plans need no defenders," and although some persons will reject the advantages of the flexibility and variability of these policies, "that is no reason for haste in governmental intervention." Starrs refers to the California legislation in support-

ing his contention that "the thrust of proposals for state compensation is predicated upon the indigency or irresponsibility of some
crime victims."[62]

While the *Minnesota Law Review* Symposium urged compensation for victims of crime, Cuba, Switzerland, New Zealand, and
the United Kingdom had already introduced compensation schemes.
California was the first American state in which the legislature
enacted compensatory assistance for victims, and, as mentioned in
the symposium, bills were introduced into both houses of the
United States Congress. "Programs designed to compensate persons
injured by crimes of violence represent in an important sense an attempt to placate a public opinion often unnerved and resentful of
what is viewed as a rising tide of aggressive criminal activity." So
says Gilbert Geis.[63] Indeed, many of the efforts that have been
made are for cooling public anger against crime, rather than for
achieving a better understanding of it. However, in addition to the
numerous "popular" demands for victim compensation, there also
appeared, mainly dating from the middle of 1965, a great number
of articles in professional journals that emphasized the importance
of the issue.[64]

Among them it may be mentioned that the issue of compensating
victims of crime was placed on the program of the National Violence Commission, and in Spring 1970 the *Southern California
Law Review* published a Symposium with Arthur J. Goldberg,
Marvin E. Wolfgang, LeRoy L. Lamborn, Stephen Schafer, Duncan Chappell, Willard A. Shank, Ralph W. Yarborough, and Kent
M. Weeks as the participants.[65]

Arthur J. Goldberg in the preface to the Symposium emphasized
that crime is a sociological and economic problem, and victims of
crime should be treated as victims of floods or hurricanes. Marvin
E. Wolfgang discussed the societal responsibility for violent behavior. LeRoy L. Lamborn examined the various remedies available to a victim of crime; citing "absorption by the victim," whereby
the victim ignores the possibility of compensation and restitution
as a remedy "by default." He proceeded to evaluate restitution by
the criminal, civil action by the victim against the criminal, and
compensation by society in the form of charity, insurance and welfare programs. Stephen Schafer discussed the problem of victim
compensation both historically and from the point of view of the
offender's responsibility; he reflected on the ancient origins of com-

pensation and restitution, which ordered satisfaction to the victim as part of the obligation of the criminal, and the genesis of modern compensation programs. Schafer again (as he did in 1958) called attention to the case for "correctional restitution," which holds the promise of both restitution to victims of crime and implementation of reformative and corrective goals in rehabilitating criminals. Duncan Chappell examined the New Zealand and Australian compensation schemes, Willard Shank analyzed the difficulties in the Californian system, and Kent M. Weeks discussed the New Zealand Criminal Injuries Compensation scheme. Senator Ralph W. Yarborough described his relentless efforts to achieve the passage of a federal victim compensation law, and claimed that as long as society continues to assume the task of preventing antisocial behavior, society will continue to owe some moral or legal obligation to the victims of crime.

In the second half of the 1960s, several states of the United States began to introduce compensation systems. California, New York, and Massachusetts were the first three, but they differed in their approach to the problem. While California incorporated compensation to victims of crime in the welfare system, New York has followed the English and New Zealand model in establishing a compensation board, and Massachusetts decided for the legalistic solution by placing the question of victim compensation under the jurisdiction of the courts. These states were the pioneers of compensation in America: many others have followed their example.

Victim Compensation in California

During the 1965 session of the California legislature, a law was enacted for the first time in the United States that provided compensatory financial assistance to victims of crimes of violence.[66] A bulletin of the California Department of Welfare states that "this is a pioneering step which California is the first state in the Union to undertake. New Zealand and Great Britain are the only other jurisdictions known to have adopted such a program."[67] Arthur J. Goldberg praised it as "beneficial legislation" and suggested that this example would be followed "throughout the country."[68] But in his detailed analysis, Childres said, "the quality of the reform fails to meet the spirit."[69]

The law itself left a number of criteria open to later decisions, and many of them found an answer in an interpretative bulletin issued a few months after the 1965 California legislature passed and the Governor signed the bill into law.[70]

First of all, it should be noted that neither the law nor the bulletin uses the terms *compensation* or *restitution,* but a so-called *aid* is to be paid "to the family of any person killed and to the victim and family, if any, of any person incapacitated as the result of a crime of violence," but only "if there is need of such aid."[71] This may be the reason why this compensation or, better, assistance has been referred to the California welfare department.

The criteria for payment are substantially the same as those provided for aid to families with dependent children, but this aid is to be paid regardless of whether the applicant meets the property qualifications prescribed for families with dependent children. For the first fiscal year (1965–1966) a maximum of $100,000 was reserved for this victim compensation scheme.

The definition of "crime of violence" is given as an act intended to do bodily harm to another, as a result of which one or more of the following has occurred:

1. A criminal complaint charging a crime of intentional bodily harm has been issued by a district attorney or federal attorney.

2. Grand jury proceedings concerning a crime of intentional bodily harm have been instituted.

3. A petition has been filed in juvenile court alleging the commission of a crime involving intentional bodily harm.

4. A report has been filed by the appropriate law enforcement agency or the coroner's office showing that a crime of intentional bodily harm has been committed, but prosecution has not been forthcoming for any of the following reasons:
    a. Perpetrator is deceased
    b. Perpetrator has not been apprehended
    c. Perpetrator was incapable of committing a crime because of age or mental condition, or the perpetrator was acting under coercion
    d. Insufficient evidence to convict the suspected perpetrator, even though the prosecuting authority is convinced that the victim was injured by a criminal act

5. The court orders the perpetrator to pay a fine to be deposited in the Indemnity Fund.[72]

The child of the victim is eligible only if he applies within five years from the time the crime was committed, and the crime was committed in California, or the injured or deceased person was a resident of California.[73]

A reinvestigation can be made not later than six months from the last investigation.[74]

Victim Compensation in New York

New York legislators addressed the idea of victim compensation, apparently because of concern with the rising rate of violent crime. The subway murder of Arthur Collins in the autumn of 1965 was one of the cases that aroused sympathy for a law to compensate victims of crime. Jurists argued for one scheme or another, and the governor of New York bitterly remarked that "the victims of violent crime are the forgotten men in our society." Finally, in spite of opposing voices (for example Gerhard O.W. Mueller suggested that the proposed legislation might promote crime), a Crime Victims Compensation Board was set up, composed of three members appointed by the governor. Indemnification was restricted to physical injury or death, and the crime had to be reported to the police in forty-eight hours.

Only in cases of serious financial hardship is compensation possible, and this again indicates the "matter of grace," rather than an assumption by the state of general responsibility for the criminal loss suffered by the victim. The act went into effect for crimes committed after October 1, 1966; the appropriation for the first fiscal year was $500,000. Thus, New York became the second victim-compensating state of the United States.

Ralph Yarborough's Federal Proposal

"In the spring of 1964, scattered newspaper references to proposals for compensating victims of crime revived the interest of Senator Ralph Yarborough in the anomaly of our concern for criminals and victims."[75] This led him to introduce appropriate legislation in the Senate, and his bill was submitted on June 17, 1965, under the number S. 2155 of the Eighty-ninth Congress, 1st Session. It was the day on which the California Assembly passed the law on aid to victims of violent crimes. Since that time, Illinois and a number of other states have started to develop legislative action, and Governor Nelson Rockefeller of New York appointed a three-man committee to produce a draft to provide victim compensation. Similar bills were introduced at this time in the House of Representatives of the Eighty-ninth Congress, 1st Session by Congresswoman Edith Green and Congressmen William D. Hathaway, Spark M. Matsugana, Jonathan B. Dingham, and George E. Brown, Jr.[76]

Yarborough suggests that "it is preferable to think of this proposal in terms of a social welfare program rather than as one establishing a true legal right." In his view, the dispensation of criminal justice and the compensation of victims should be separated: "In compensating the victims, we do not want the criminal guilt of the defendant to be an issue."

The Yarborough proposal, in parts reminiscent of the New Zealand compensation scheme, limits the crime-range to crimes causing personal injury. It rejects an extension to property loss in view of high cost and the probable protection by private insurance. Criminal acts compensable under this bill are listed by offenses, derived from the District of Columbia Code and the United States Code, and include every type of violent crime that might result in compensable injury.

The bill sets the maximum compensation at $25,000, and an award to a victim may be made whether or not any person is ever prosecuted or convicted of a crime, and even if, by reason of age or insanity, the perpetrator cannot be classified as a criminal.

Senator Yarborough suggests the establishment of a Violent Crimes Compensation Commission, which would be composed of three members appointed by the President. No member would be permitted to engage in any other business, vocation, or employment. In order to carry out the provisions of the proposed act, the commission would hold such hearings, would sit and act at such times and places, and would take such testimony as the commission deemed advisable. Orders and decisions of the commission would be final, but the commission would be empowered to institute an action against the offender for the recovery of the whole or any part of the compensation.[77]

Victim Compensation in Massachusetts

The Massachusetts program to compensate victims of violent crimes, as it has been correctly pointed out by Herbert Edelhertz and Gilbert Geis, is markedly different from other schemes in the United States of America or Canada.[78] Aside from the systems in Northern Ireland and Australia, this appears to be the only one where the lower judiciary and the attorney general of the state fill in the roles played in other countries and states by administrative agencies (such as the board, or welfare offices). The Massachusetts program is to be noted also because it fortifies one of the Recommendations of the 1973 First International Symposium on Victimology: the public awareness of the program, as far as one can judge from the number of applicants and random personal interviews, was and is inordinately low. The existence and operation of such schemes should be widely disseminated among the public.

A special commission on victim compensation was created in 1966 by a resolution of the Senate and the House of Representatives of the Commonwealth of Massachusetts. This commission held a public hearing on June 6, 1967. The victim compensation system was enacted in the 1967 legislature, and has been in operation since July 1, 1968.

After the public hearing, the special commission released a report[79] that listed the arguments for victim compensation systems:[80]

1. *Legal Obligation*—This is perhaps the most popular and forceful argument; it bases compensation on the state's "failure to protect" its individual members: since the state forbids a victim to take the law into his own hands, it is obligated to recover damages for him after failing to protect him. This idea is not new and not a radical departure from prevailing political and legal norms.

2. *Social Welfare*—Just as modern democracy dictates public assistance for the disabled veteran, the sick, the unemployed, and the aged, so should public assistance be afforded the suffering victim of crime. The argument rests not on any inherent obligation of the state, but rather on the modern conscience, which cannot stomach the misery of the helpless.

3. *Grace of the Government*—This plan mirrors the merciful intervention of the state in individual cases, in contrast to the "social welfare" view, which deals with whole classes or categories of people.

4. *Crime Prevention*—This point of view emphasizes compensation for "Good Samaritans" injured in attempting to aid victims or

the police. According to this argument, a compensation plan for those injured while attempting to help enforce the law might encourage citizen assistance and prevent certain crimes.

5. *Political Reasons*—The articulators of political opinion enthusiastically endorse the concept of compensation. "This," they say, "is what the people want."

6. *Anti-alienation*—This compensation argument points to the disillusionment of victimized individuals who have suffered not only criminal injury but also, as a consequence of their desire to cooperate with the prosecution, the insult of losses of time and income.

None of these arguments, however, presents the case for restitution by the offender as a correctional principle employing his personal obligation. All victim compensation systems of the last decade have one characteristic in common: they are governed by the spirit of damages and do not aim at any restitutive correctional goal. Even in this narrow context, the eventual inclusion of any compensation program in the *criminal* law code would be an achievement.

The Commonwealth of Massachusetts, in its "Act to Provide for the Compensation of Victims of Violent Crimes,"[81] has provided that compensation awards should be determined by the state district courts. This program extends compensation only to those victims who have suffered injury or harm by crimes involving "the application of force or violence, or the threat of force or violence by the offender," thus excluding injuries arising from the operation of a motor vehicle. The victim and, in case of his death, dependents of the victim are eligible for compensation. The origin of the idea that makes the courts responsible for the operation of the compensation system is found in the Commonwealth's Constitution, which provides the right of every subject "to find a certain remedy by having recourse to the laws for all injuries or wrongs." It has also been argued that questions of victim compensation "involve a broad consideration of more intangible social and ethical factors" and that "the courts are most expert" in this area.[82] Also, judges trained in the traditions of the common law have over the years proven their effectiveness in matters of fact finding and adjudication. As the Massachusetts Special Commission states, "law as developed in our common law courts today is something created with the interests of society in mind, through which the individual can find a means of securing his interest, so far as society recognizes them."[83]

The claim for compensation under the Massachusetts program is first filed in a district court. The same judge may not hear both the compensation claim and the criminal case on which that claim is based. The claim must be filed not later than one year after the commission of crime, or not later than ninety days after the death of the victim, whichever is earlier. The State Attorney General is notified of the filing of the compensation claim by the clerk of the court. The Attorney General's role is an adversary one—he has investigative authority and may present supporting or opposing information to the court. The claimant is responsible for presenting his own evidence, but may be represented by counsel. Under the Massachusetts program, no compensation is to be paid unless the claimant has, as a result of the injury, expended at least one hundred dollars or lost two continuous weeks of earnings or support. The total compensable injury is limited to out-of-pocket expenses plus the loss of earnings or support; there is an absolute ceiling of ten thousand dollars.

In determining the amount of compensation, the court may take into account any conduct on the part of the victim that may have contributed to the infliction of his injury. The amount of compensation may be denied entirely or reduced proportionately in light of such conduct. Such conduct may be disregarded where the victim's injury resulted from efforts to aid another victim, to assist in crime prevention, or to apprehend a person who has in fact committed a felony or a crime in the victim's presence. Any award of compensation is to be reduced by the amount of payments received from the offender, insurance program benefits, or other public funds. Thus, in Massachusetts the victim's responsibility is taken into consideration.

In Massachusetts, a fund is set up to provide the necessary monies. Once the state satisfies the judgement, it may itself proceed against the offender for restitution. The existence of indemnity illustrates the state's concern for the victim's well-being, which rests on a "failure to protect" rationale.[84]

Victim Compensation in Other American States

Hawaii was the fourth state in the United States where a system of compensating victims of crime was introduced.[85] The three-member Criminal Injuries Compensation Commission succeeded in establishing a compensation scheme in 1968. This program differs in several respects from other American systems.[86] First, it is not necessary for the victims to prove that they are in financial hardship or need; second, Hawaii seems to have the only compensation program that permits indemnification for "pain and suffering"; and third, at least to 1972, Hawaii allows collateral recovery —for example, the victim can receive both workmen's compensation and victim compensation at the same time. "Pain and suffering" are compensated, in spite of the difficulties this presents, because Hawaii wanted to offer to each qualified applicant a fair and equitable award. There is no need to give evidence of financial hardship because, as the original bill phrased it, Hawaii proposes compensation awards not as a benevolent grant on the basis of mercy or sympathy, as an acknowledgement of the government's duty to protect its people from the consequences of crime. The double recovery was permitted with the logic that an extra insurance cannot effect compensation for criminal acts.

In 1968 Maryland became the fifth state where victim compensation jurisdiction was established, followed in 1969 by Nevada, and in 1971 by New Jersey, all of which followed the British model of procedure. In 1972 Alaska and Rhode Island introduced legislative measures for compensating victims of crime, and Washington followed suit in 1973. Many states have encountered difficulties in persuading their legislators to accept the idea of victim compensation: Connecticut, Florida, and Illinois, for example, have been trying since the mid-1960s to adopt compensation measures.

Victim Compensation on the Federal Level

The federal government is not behind those states where legislative efforts for compensating victims of crime have failed. Senator Yarborough's pioneering proposal made compensation a popular issue among legislators, yet the Congress failed again-and-again to pass a law that would provide for compensating victims of crime. After Ralph W. Yarborough lost his "battle for a Federal Violent Crimes Compensation Act,"[87] many other senators introduced similar bills; in fact, at one point three senators submitted bills within twenty-four hours of each other, but all remained only bills. Among others, United States Senators Alan Bible from Nevada,

Robert C. Byrd from West Virginia, Vance Hartke from Indiana, Edward M. Kennedy from Massachusetts, Mike Mansfield from Montana, Walter F. Mondale from Minnesota, and John L. Mc-Clellan from Arkansas submitted bills to provide for the compensation of innocent victims of violent crime who are in need, to make grants to states for the payment of such compensation, to authorize an insurance program and death and disability benefits for public safety officers, to provide civil remedies for victims or racketeering activity and for similar other purposes. Many other senators have joined with those who proposed these legislative measures, or co-sponsored the bills, or at least supported the idea of compensating victims of violent crimes.[88]

In the First Session of the Ninety-second Congress, in 1971 and 1972, an extensive hearing took place before the Subcommittee on Criminal Laws and Procedures of the Committee on the Judiciary in the United States Senate; the record of this hearing was published in a 1,112-page volume.[89] It should be noted that among the great many testimonies, statements, and exhibits, only three academicians were invited to personally testify: these were James Brooks, from the New Mexico State University, Paul F. Rothstein, from the Georgetown University Law Center, and Stephen Schafer, from Northeastern University.

Diversion Programs and Victim Compensation: Victim Advocates

A kind of compensation to victims of crime may be recognized in the *diversion programs,* the seed of which can be found in a recommendation of the President's National Crime Commission that proposed directing the offender to community resources as a sort of substitute for incarceration.[90] The popularity of the idea (which, incidentally, is loaded with unrecognized and unsolved theoretical problems and difficulties) has caused diversion to be submitted to explorations on police level, pretrial level, postconvictional level, and parole board level.[91] Of these four levels, the pretrial diversion and the postconvictional diversion are very close to restitution and compensation.

Pretrial diversion was recommended by the First International Symposium on Victimology in 1973, and one of its pioneering experiments in Florida made use of victims' Ombudsmen. Boston, Massachusetts, followed, in 1975, where at the Dorchester District

Court the ombudsmen are called *victim advocates* and *mediation panels*. This diversion is actually hardly more than professionalized charity, where the sufferer-victim is helped by a variety of advisors —the victim advocates—who guide him to the right agencies to mitigate his psychological, financial, and medical needs and pains. In terms of welfare, it is reminiscent of the strongly criticized California compensation system, except that instead of financial assistance, advice is given. Somewhat more meaningful is the role of the mediation panels, which try to bring about a sort of agreement between the criminal and his victim that may guide the court in making its decision in the criminal case. As a matter of course, even the successful bargaining of these mediation panels is not binding on the sentencing of the court.

Postconvictional diversion was first attempted by the Minnesota Restitution Center (originated in 1969 by the PORT—the Probationed Offenders Rehabilitation and Training project of Olmsted County in Rochester, Minnesota), and was partially supported by the Minnesota Governor's Commission on Crime Prevention and Control.[92] This center, as Burt Galaway and Joe Hudson contended, is the first exploration of implementing the use of an offender-victim scheme within the context of a community-based residential facility. The Restitution Center diverts selected criminals out of the prison to a restitution focused parole status during the fourth month of their incarceration. The offender and the victim are brought together and are supposed to enter into a contractual agreement. The program staff functions as a third party both in helping the negotiations and, following parole, in facilitating the completion of the agreement by helping the offender to obtain and maintain work and by supervising the terms of the contract. The basic idea for this may have been taken from Stephen Schafer's idea of punitive restitution in 1958,[93] although his proposal was more tightly binding and excluded all social welfare aspects. The Minnesota Restitution Center started its operation in September 1972, and within its limits and burdened by theoretical difficulties it appears to operate successfully.

General Perspectives of the Compensation and Restitution Problem

"The guilty man lodged, fed, clothed, warmed, lighted, entertained, at the expense of the state in a model cell, issued from it with a sum of money lawfully earned, has paid his debt to society; he can set his victims at defiance; but the victim has his consolation; he can think that by taxes he pays to the Treasury, he has contributed towards the paternal care, which has guarded the criminal during his stay in prison."[94] These were the bitter and sarcastic words of Prins, the Belgian representative, at the Paris Prison Congress in 1895, when, during a discussion of the problem of restitution to victims of crime, he could no longer contain his indignation at various practical and theoretical objections that were raised to his proposals on behalf of the victim.

His was not the first voice demanding recognition and respect for the victim and his injury, and it was by no means the last. Adherents of classic criminal law increasingly voiced their concern, but the fact was that "the unfortunate victim of criminality was habitually ignored" right up to the present time.[95]

Attention has frequently been called to the hardship that ensues after a person is attacked by a criminal, but less attention has been called to the pain of the punishment that ensues when an offender is brought to justice for a crime precipitated by his victim. This twofold problem is not simple. It involves several practical and theoretical complications, and requires multidirectional research. Not pity for the victim, but appreciation of his claim is needed. Not thirst for revenge against the criminal, but a clearer understanding of his deed and that of his victim is needed to help reform and rehabilitate him. The punitive or correctional restitution (should it be work, personal service, or payment to the victim), to be meted out by the criminal court, and not the charitable or insurance kind of compensation (to be arranged by mediating agencies with civil characteristics), might be the answer.

NOTES

1. See details in Stephen Schafer, *Restitution to Victims of Crime* (London and Chicago, 1960), pp. 101–8, or 2nd enlarged ed., under the title *Compensation and Restitution to Victims of Crime* (Montclair, N.J., 1970), pp. 101–8.

2. Margery Fry, "Justice for Victims," *The Observer* (London, July 7, 1957).

3. "Compensation for Victims of Criminal Violence, a Round Table," *Journal of Public Law,* 8 (Atlanta, 1959), 191–253.

4. Ibid., p. 202. Fred E. Inbau is quoted.

5. Ibid., pp. 209–10. Henry Weihofen is quoted.

6. Ibid., pp. 229–30. Gerhard O.W. Mueller is quoted.

7. Schafer, *Restitution.*

8. R.E. Prentice, M.P., *Bill* 33, November 11, 1959.

9. *Compensation for Victims of Crimes of Violence,* Home Office (London, June 1961), Cmnd. 1406.

10. *Compensation for Victims of Crimes of Violence,* Home Office (London, March 1964), Cmnd. 2323.

11. Letter of H.B. Wilson, *Home Office* (London, August 7, 1964).

12. Marvin E. Wolfgang, *Patterns in Criminal Homicide* (Philadelphia, 1958), p. 26.

13. Act No. 134, October 25, 1963.

14. Bruce J. Cameron, "Compensation for Victims of Crime: the New Zealand Experiment," *Journal of Public Law,* 12 (1963), 367–75.

15. Letter of J.L. Robson, Secretary for Justice, Department of Justice (Wellington, January 20, 1966).

16. Kathleen J. Smith, *A Cure for Crime: The Case for the Self Determinate Prison Sentence* (London, 1965). The basic idea appeared in an article in *The Spectator* in 1964.

17. Herbert Spencer, *Essais de morale de science et d'esthétique: Essais de politique,* II (4th ed., Paris, 1898), VIII, *Morale de la prison,* p. 352.

18. Raffaele Garofalo, *Criminology,* trans. R.W. Millar (Boston, 1914), pp. 419–35. This differs somewhat from his proposal to the Paris Prison Congress in 1895. There he suggested that instead of going to prison, the man should work for the state, retaining for himself only enough to keep from starving. The rest would go into a "caisse d'épargne" for the reparation of the wrong. *The Paris Prison Congress, 1895,* Summary Report (London, n.d.).

19. Samuel J. Barrows, *The Sixth International Congress, Brussels, 1900, Report of Its Proceedings and Conclusions* (Washington, 1903), p. 52.

20. Carlo Waeckerling, *Die Sorge für den Verletzten im Strafrecht* (Zürich, 1946), p. 130.

21. Schafer, *Restitution,* pp. 128–29.

22. Albert Eglash, "Creative Restitution, Some Suggestions for Prison Rehabilitation Programs," *American Journal of Correction,* 6 (November-December 1958), 20–34.

23. Claude Baumann, *Die Stellung des Geschädigen im schwezerischen Strafprocess* (Aarau, 1958), p. 5.

24. *Schweiz, Strafgesetzbuch* (StGB), Swiss Penal Code of December 21, 1937, Arts. 60 (1), 60 (2), pp. 376–78.

25. Information supplied by Erwin R. Frey, Professor of the University of Zürich.

26. Cameron, "Compensation for Victims," p. 367.

27. Act No. 134, October 25, 1963.

28. New Zealand Parliamentary Debate 1865 (1963); as quoted by Cameron, "Compensation for Victims," p. 370.

29. Criminal Injuries Compensation Act 1963, Arts. 2, 4, 10–16, 17 and Schedule, 18–19.

30. *Report on Operation of the Criminal Injuries Compensation Act 1963, to December 31, 1965;* in personal communication from J.L. Robson, Secretary for Justice, Wellington, January 20, 1966.

31. Ibid., p. 1.

32. Criminal Injuries Compensation Act 1963, Arts. 23–26.

33. *Report on Operation of Criminal Injuries Compensation,* p. 2.

34. Henry Brooke, Home Secretary (in the debate in the House of Commons), *Hansard,* Vol. 694, No. 103, col. 1127.

35. Lord Dilhorne, Lord Chancellor (in the debate in the House of Lords), *Hansard,* Vol. 257, No. 72, col. 1354.

36. Brooke, *Hansard,* col. 1128.

37. Ibid., col. 1132.

38. R.E. Prentice (in the debate in the House of Commons), *Hansard,* Vol. 694, No. 103, col. 1187.

39. "Penal Practice in a Changing Society," British Home Secretary's White Paper presented to Parliament (February, 1959), Cmnd. 2323, p. 4.

40. Bernard W.M. Downey, "Compensating Victims of Violent Crime," *British Journal of Criminology,* Vol. 5, No. 1 (July 1964).

41. Bishop of Chester (in the debate in the House of Lords), *Hansard,* Vol. 245, col. 269. Cited by Downey, "Compensating Victims."

42. *The Scheme,* official publication of the Home Office, amended in August 1965, paragraphs 1, 4–7, 12, 20.

43. Ibid., revised par. 17; "Notes on Procedure," Criminal Injuries Compensation Board, Hearings Before Three Members of the Board, C.I.C.B. 14, par. 1 (1) *et seq;* "Notes on Procedure," Criminal Injuries Compensation Board, letter of the Home Office, January 18, 1966.

44. *First Report and Accounts,* Criminal Injuries Compensation Board, presented to Parliament in October 1965 (London, April 30, 1965), Cmnd. 2782.

45. Home Office, December 31, 1965 (Mimeographed).

46. Ibid., pp. 1–9.

47. See more of the Australian system in Louis Waller, "Compensating the Victims of Crime in Australia and New Zealand," and Uzy Hasson and Leslie Sebba, "Compensation to Victims of Crime: A Comparative Survey," both unpublished papers, Xeroxed, presented to the *First International Symposium on Victimology,* September 2–6, 1973, Jerusalem.

48. Tuija Mäkinen, *Rikosvahinkojen Korvaukset* (Helsinki, 1975), pp. 64–66; and personal information from Inkeri Anttila, Kauko Aromaa, and Matti Joutsen in the Research Institute of Legal Policy in Helsinki in 1975.

49. "Act Concerning Compensation from Public Funds for Victims of Criminal Acts," art. 8, *Ministry of Justice,* Helsinki, Finland, official preliminary translation, pp. 2–3, unpublished, Xeroxed.

50. See details in the special number of the Bulletin of the International Asso-

ciation of Penal Law, *Revue Internationale de Droit Pénal,* 44: 1st and 2nd trimesters, Nos. 1 and 2, 1973, pp. 5–416.

51. December 1964, Montreal, Canada.

52. Thorsten Sellin and Marvin E. Wolfgang, *The Measurement of Delinquency* (New York, 1964).

53. Gerhard O.W. Mueller, "Compensation for Victims of Crime: Thought Before Action," *Minnesota Law Review,* 50 (December 1965), 213.

54. Gerhard O.W. Mueller, Marvin E. Wolfgang, Stephen Schafer, Ralph W. Yarborough, Robert D. Childres, and James E. Starrs, "Compensation to Victims of Crime of Personal Violence: An Examination of the Scope of the Problem, A Symposium," *Minnesota Law Review,* 50 (December 1965), 212.

55. Ibid., pp. 214, 215, 218, 221.

56. Marvin E. Wolfgang, "Victim Compensation in Crimes of Personal Violence," *Minnesota Law Review,* 50 (December 1965), 230, 234.

57. Sellin and Wolfgang, *Measurement of Delinquency.*

58. Wolfgang, "Victim Compensation," pp. 240, 241.

59. Stephen Schafer, "Restitution to Victims of Crime—An Old Correctional Aim Modernized," *Minnesota Law Review,* 50 (December 1965), 245, 249, 251, 254.

60. Ralph W. Yarborough, "S. 2155 of the Eighty-ninth Congress—The Criminal Injuries Compensation Act," *Minnesota Law Review,* 50 (December 1965), 255, 256.

61. Robert Childres, "Compensation for Criminally Inflicted Personal Injury," *Minnesota Law Review,* 50 (December 1965), 278, 281, 282.

62. James E. Starrs, "A Modest Proposal to Insure Justice for Victims of Crime," *Minnesota Law Review,* 50 (December 1965), 305, 309, 310.

63. Gilbert Geis, "State Aid to Victims of Violent Crime," report to the President's National Crime Commission 1966, p. 1. (Mimeographed).

64. *Albany Law Review,* June 1966, pp. 325–33; *American Bar Association Journal,* March 1966, pp. 237–39; *Harvard Law Review,* June 1965, pp. 1683–86; *Northwestern Law Review,* March-April 1966, pp. 72–104; *Notre Dame Lawyer,* April 1966, pp. 487–506; *Saint Louis University Law Journal,* 10: 1965, pp. 238–50; *Stanford Law Review,* November 1965, pp. 266–73; *Texas Law Review,* November 1965, pp. 38–54; *University of Chicago Law Review,* Spring 1966, pp. 531–57; *Vanderbilt Law Review,* December 1965, pp. 220–28, and many others.

65. *Symposium: Governmental Compensation for Victims of Violence, Southern California Law Review,* Vol. 41, No. 1, 1970, pp. 1–121.

66. Cal. Stat. Ch. 1549, An act to add Section 1500.02 to the Welfare and Institutions Code and to add Section 11211 to Division 9 of the Welfare and Institutions Code as proposed by Assembly Bill No. 1682, relating to aid families with dependent children. Passed by the Assembly June 17, 1965.

67. *Department Bulletin,* State of California, Health and Welfare Agency No. 648 (Sacramento, December 8, 1965), Chap. I.

68. *The New York Times,* July 24, 1965.

69. Childres, "Compensation for Criminally Inflicted Personal Injury," p. 279.

70. *Department Bulletin,* Chaps. II–VIII.

71. *Welfare and Institutions Code,* Act, Section I, Section 1500.02.

72. *Department Bulletin,* Chap. II.

73. Ibid., Chap. IV.

74. Ibid., Chap. VI.

75. Yarborough, "S. 2155 of the Eighty-ninth Congress," p. 255.

76. *The New York Times,* October 24, 1965, p. 1.

77. Yarborough, "S. 2155 of the Eighty-ninth Congress," pp. 256, 257, 261–64, 266–70.

78. Herbert Edelhertz and Gilbert Geis, *Public Compensation to Victims of Crime* (New York, 1974), p. 107.

79. *Report of the Special Commission on the Compensation of Victims of Violent Crimes,* Commonwealth of Massachusetts, House 5151, July 1967.

80. See Stephen Schafer, "The Proper Role of a Victim-Compensation System," *Crime and Delinquency,* Vol. 21, No. 1, Jan. 1975, p. 48.

81. *Massachusetts General Laws,* Chap. 258A (Supp. 1968).

82. *Report,* p. 16.

83. Ibid., pp. 16–17.

84. This justification seems to have underlain the pre-revolution Cuban system, *Codigo de Defensa Social* (Code of Social Defense) of 1938, Arts. 110–111. This Code was substituted, as the criminal legislation, for the ancient Spanish Code in force since 1879.

85. *Hawaii Revised Statutes,* 351-1, 1968.

86. See Edelhertz and Geis, *Public Compensation,* pp. 130–153.

87. Ralph W. Yarborough, "The Battle for a Federal Violent Crimes Compensation Act: The Genesis of S.9," *Southern California Law Review,* Vol. 41, No. 1, 1970, p. 99.

88. Some of these senators are: J. Caleb Boggs (Delaware), Quentin N. Burdick (North Dakota), Marlow W. Cook (Kentucky), James O. Eastland (Mississippi), Robert P. Griffin (Michigan), Clifford P. Hansen (Wyoming), Ernest F. Hollings (South Carolina), Roman L. Hruska (Nebraska), Hubert Humphrey (Minnesota), Lee Metcalf (Montana), Frank E. Moss (Utah), William V. Roth, Jr. (Delaware), and Strom Thurmond (South Carolina).

89. *Victims of Crime,* Hearing before the Subcommittee on Criminal Laws and Procedures of the Committee on the Judiciary, United States Senate, Ninety-second Congress, First Session (printed for the use of the Committee on the Judiciary, United States Government Printing Office, Washington, D.C., 1972).

90. *The Challenge of Crime in a Free Society,* Report of the President's Commission on Law Enforcement and Administration of Justice (Washington, D.C., 1967), p. 134.

91. Joe Hudson, Burt Galaway, William Henschel, Jay Lindgren, and Jon Penton, "Diversion Programming in Criminal Justice: The Case of Minnesota," *Federal Probation,* Vol. XXXIX, No. 1 (March, 1975), pp. 11–19.

92. See details in Burt Galaway and Joe Hudson, "Issues in the Correctional Implementation of Restitution to Victims of Crime," in Joe Hudson and Burt Galaway, eds., *Considering the Victim: Readings in Restitution and Victim Compensation* (Springfield, Ill., 1975), pp. 351–60.

93. Stephen Schafer, *Compensation and Restitution to Victims of Crime* (2nd enlarged ed., Montclair, N.J., 1970).

94. *Summary Report,* The Paris Prison Congress (London, 1895).

95. William Tallack, *Reparation to the Injured and the Rights of the Victim of Crime to Compensation* (London, 1900), pp. 10–11.

4

The Functional Responsibility

The Problem of Responsibility

In the matter of criminal-victim relationships, alarm and indignation was directed for a long time exclusively against the offender; this was coupled with indifference toward the victim's role. Now the importance of the victim's role is gaining in acceptance, but only slowly. Certainly, ever since Archimedes sacrificed a hundred oxen to the gods, people have been fearful of recognizing new truths. The outlook is worsened by the fact that the problem of criminal-victim relationships is essentially a problem of responsibility, and this intricate issue is indeed not a favored topic in modern criminological thinking. Van Hamel, who introduced the term "criminal-etiology" at the congress in Hamburg in 1905 warned that progress in solving the crime problem depends upon a better understanding of "responsibility."

However, in the analysis of crime in the twentieth century, the concept of responsibility is far too often evaded by looking only at the *causa proxima*. Criminology has yet to find its Newton or its Kepler, and the more we try to go forward, the more we have to realize how backward we are. It would seem that for a few decades the focus of research has been limited to the matter of judging, patterning, and treating those who are *responsible* for a crime. It has not been concerned with what this responsibility means; responsibility is handled as if it were some antecedent postulate.

Responsibility has always been and always will be a crucial issue of the crime problem. Even representatives of the radical wings of criminology, like the naturalist Lombroso or the socialist Ferri, who fought for half a century for substituting the terms *danger* and *sanctions* for *guilt* and *punishment,* had to recognize this basic element of crime. In more recent history, the highly subjective and almost apocalyptic Soviet criminal law brought the socialistic societal interpretation of responsibility into special prominence. In general, and regardless of ideology, in all societies the conceptualization of responsibility has proved to be the force that shapes the approach to problems of crime. The concept of responsibility has fluctuated bewilderingly from society to society, and from one generation to the next. At least since the Renaissance, Europeans have been very much aware of the inconsistencies in appraising its role, inasmuch as this role decides the distinction between conformists and criminals. Roscoe Pound said that "the ultimate basis of delictal liability is the social interest in the general security."[1]

Indeed, the entire history of criminal procedures evidences the differing approaches to a definition of responsibility. In the pursuit of the "general security," any particular definition of responsibility has not always seemed right to all the members of the society concerned. Who is responsible, for what, and why? This is the question that must be answered if we are to reach an understanding of crime rates, gang delinquency, sex offenses, organized crime, and all other topical crime problems, among them criminal-victim relationships. Responsibility will never be perfectly conceptualized or understood. However, its significance in the analysis of crime lies in the very fact that it is a relative matter. It is an ever-changing formula. Crime does not change, but responsibility does.

Generally speaking, responsibility is not an isolated factor at any given time. It is an instrument of social control used at all times by all societies in order to help maintain themselves. In this context, it explains crime and relates criminals to conformists in spatial, cultural, and time dimensions. In a given social system, responsibility is functional because it helps to secure and maintain group order. Defined as an ever-changing formula, it explains crime and relates criminals to conformists from the standpoint of a particular system. It has a bearing, in fact, on most crimes. It reflects their etiology as projected to the functional role of the participants in a crime. If responsibility is functional, it cannot operate inside an isolated and objectivized area of stiff formalism. It goes beyond the boundaries of the offender's personality and beyond the boundaries of strict legal definitions of criminal offenses. Functional responsibility is widespread and touches upon the functional forces of crime, among them the criminal-victim relationship.

Since the concept of functional responsibility tends to embrace not only traditional factors, but others as well, this comprehensive view cannot avoid such questions as causality, free will or justice in law. These problems are obstacles to a meaningful conceptualization of responsibility. In fact, nearly every aspect of the crime problem requires one stand or another on these problems in order to establish a theoretical proposition.[2] This book does not attempt to present general theories for these insoluble mysteries; it is far less ambitious. However, it should provide some understanding of the concept of functional responsibility.

The Limitations of Free Will by Responsibilities

The problem of free will is one of the most difficult problems of philosophy, yet one of the most popular. The debate on the controversial issue of determinism versus indeterminism is interminable. Acceptance of an unlimited application of the law of causality would be as grandiose an hypothesis as would acceptance of free will as a metaphysical concept only.

Determinism, the theory that we have no free choice and that our actions are determined only by external forces, annihilates the concept of a human will. In other words, determinism says that will does not motivate action, but that action results automatically from outside causes. In a way, however, indeterminism leads to a similar result: a will that is not involved in any way with causal reality would be only an illusion. Johannes Buridan's donkey, mentioned by Schopenhauer, Windelband, Gomperz, and others in the literature, clearly illustrates the complexities of opinions and can be used both to defend and to attack both views. This hungry donkey stands between two haystacks, equally fragrant, equal in size, and at equal distances away. The poor animal, having no will to decide (if the deterministic view is right), or having no motives to influence its decision (if the indeterministic view is right), eventually reaches a condition of absolute indifference and, being unable to choose one of the haystacks, simply dies of hunger. Incidentally, this classic story of the donkey may indicate that the validity of one's conclusion rests upon what he actually understands by the terms that are used.

Since new theories sooner or later generally prove to be merely versions of long-forgotten old theories, the chances are that *the* solution of the problem will not be easily discovered. Thus, from a practical viewpoint, useful answers contain a mixture of both the indeterministic and the deterministic, and differ mainly in terms of how much of each. Such a compromise may also have been necessary because there is no philosophical guarantee either that adherents of the indeterministic view possess freedom of will in coming to their conclusion or that adherents of the deterministic thesis express their judgment only as mouthpieces of external forces.

The philosophy of all penal systems seems at first to be heavily indeterministic. The idea of official punishment itself indicates the lawmaker's assumption that the criminal has freedom of choice. Criminal law assumes that man is free and able to form a "more or less impartial judgment of the alternative actions" and can act "in accordance with that judgment."[3] It would be senseless, so the argument runs, to offer a choice between reward and punishment if free will were not a fact. After all, criminal responsibility is based on the choice to commit a criminal act. Criminal law operates on the presumption that man is an intelligent and reasoning creature who can recognize values. In other words, only those can be punished who *want* a crime. At least, this is the case when the penal system applies retributive punishment. Nobody can seriously dispute the point that in our penal systems, with respect to correction and rehabilitation, nothing has set aside the concepts of guilt, retribution, and deterrence.

However, this apparent freedom is not always as free as it appears. In reality, it involves only a limited range of choices, and in these choices there is only a limited number of alternatives. Even here, biological needs may play a part in determining the action. But Kantian dualism does not fit in with any mixture of deterministic and indeterministic elements; the realistic human will can exist alone neither in the causal nature nor in the intellect. No moderate deterministic or moderate indeterministic thinking can accept the existence of man's two worlds as separate entities: the *mundus sensibilis* and the *mundus intelligibilis*. Man's position in the functioning universe demands the merger of these two worlds. The actual culture of these merged worlds molds both the causal reality and the intellect and joins them in a single unity. This culture is not some "third Reich," as Heinrich Rickert called it; it is not a third self-contained world that is linked with the other two.[4] Furthermore, it has no connection with Hegel's strict historical and social causality, where the realities of nature, "the unsolved contradiction," cannot find their comfortable place.[5]

Culture, and the socialization processes that go with it, as they are being discussed here, both saturate and limit the individual will. It is the actual world in which the individual lives and functions, and he learns to do so through the ordinary socializing processes. Cultural values not only are built into the person, but also build his personality and thus limit his choices and set his alternatives, and the freedom of man's will develops only after these values have been indoctrinated with him. The socializing processes develop bias and prejudice, likes and dislikes, beliefs and disbeliefs, affirmations and negations concerning the basic and guiding issues of the world in which man exists and functions, often influencing even less overt layers of this world. Culture, through socialization, "eventually results in making the person what he is."[6] Man actively masters his culture, but only after he passively accepts it.

Except where physical necessities, which prevail throughout the material universe, rigidly dictate human action, our faculty of knowing, reasoning, and choosing is considerably arrested by indoctrination in our culture. Even some biological phenomena can be controlled to some extent by cultural forces. The ideas of a culture are infused into a person before his faculties of knowing, reasoning, and choosing have had a chance to develop to maturity. Therefore, these faculties—all related to the will—are no longer really free. The person knows, reasons, and makes his choices, but normally what he would will to know, how he would will to reason, and what choices he would will to make are acts of the will that are imbued with and limited by the ideas of his culture. This is why the more a person is socialized, the more likely he is to be a conformist. Socialization and resocialization are operational concepts in the service of the problem of free will.

Sartre's cynical remark that "I am responsible for everything, in fact, except for my very responsibility" may be recommended as a motto for those who argue strongly against the idea of retribution in modern penal systems.[7] The free but culturally imbued and limited human will is, in fact, the profile of the functional responsibility. Culture not only establishes the direction and range of knowing, reasoning, and choosing, but also wants man to use these faculties actively and functionally—in the indicated direction and within the indicated range. While there are limits on the freedom of the will, it is expected that what freedom there is will be used. Man is made responsible for functioning outside (trespassing) the approved limits on the freedom of his will. At the same time, he has the responsibility for making his will function within the approved limits in order to promote his culture. Man's self-imposed limitations on his freedom of will create responsibility in him for his functional role in his world.

When man functions within his limited freedom, this is expected, possibly rewarded; when he functions outside the limits on his freedom, this is resented, possibly punished. This does not mean that all less-adequately socialized persons, who as a result feel less restricted in their freedom of will, are necessarily criminals. This is the case even if opportunity enables their free will to choose an illegitimate alternative. However, unlimited freedom of the will creates the possibility of full revolt against the majority who will the world as it should be, according to their culturally imbued and limited knowledge, reasons, and choices.

At the same time, man is not condemned to passivity. Inertia is not one of his characteristics, and to see him in a state of rest or to see him in motion caused only by external forces would belie experience. Moreover, he is supposed to use his knowledge, reason, and ability to choose in order to safeguard, improve, and perpetuate his culture. He is expected to be free and functional, and he can be made responsible for that. Man has goals and aspirations, he is taught to have them and use them, but only for his culture and not against its values. His functional role extends as far as the limitations of his actual freedom of will. These limitations do not exclude his experiencing, they only arrest his evaluation of his social responsibilities. The list of active duties in his functional role is almost endless.

Compared to those who criminally trespass (who go beyond the culture's limitations on their freedom of will), his functional role is to prevent a choice that will result in criminal trespassing. The victim's role is to prevent his own victimization; this is one of his functional responsibilities.

The Rightness of Law

A culturally imbued and limited free will, based on functional responsibility, testifies to the fact that we are free in our actions, yet we are not taught what we need to know or learn, but what we have to know in order to participate in our particular cultural group. The actual power structure of this group defines the values to be learned and establishes the degree to which the will is to be imbued and limited by the culture. The existence and operation of any power structure may well lead to the development of an opposing structure that may be capable ultimately of taking it over and of changing the cultural value system in part or as a whole. The dynamics of such a change would depend largely on the potential of those who are inadequately socialized, and who may thus use their greater freedom of will to obtain knowledge, engage in reasoning, and make choices outside the culturally imbued and limited area. The change may also depend on the degree of discomfort caused by the new values introduced by the opposing power structure, which those under the original power structure cannot comprehend because of the limitations on their knowledge and reasoning.

When such an upheaval is successful, a new value system and new norms may be created, and the old values may be rejected or reversed. In this case, an extension of the socialization (or resocialization) is unavoidable. However, as long as the existing social power prevails, the original goals and aspirations obtain, whether available or blocked; ideas and beliefs are fortified; limitations on the freedom of the will do not change; roles continue with the same assigned functional responsibilities. In other words, continued socialization takes place in accordance with the cultural values of the existing power. Since man's will is not entirely free and is culturally imbued, aspirations and goals are seen as legitimate, approved barriers to them as justifiable, and roles as constructive.

The criminal or the delinquent, however, is roleless, and violates the norms because he has not been adequately socialized to accept the value system of the ruling social power; the freedom of his will was not adequately limited, or his knowledge, reason, and choosing were not adequately imbued with cultural values. His functional role and the applicable legal norms have not "come through" to him. His crime or delinquency is, thus, not necessarily an act of opposition against this norm-forming power, because he does not know and hence cannot judge these values. Rather, the law, in a cultural context, appears to him as an alien and external phenomenon with which he is unfamiliar and whose rationale is incomprehensible.

Crime or delinquency seen in terms of revolt against the social power, say against the middle class, makes sense only if the criminal or the delinquent understands the values on which the norms are based. In most instances, he knows the formal norms and is aware of what can and cannot be done, but because he lacks adequate "cultural saturation," he cannot be acquainted with the values underlying the norms. He knows the *formal* prohibitions and rationalizes his own deviance. The victim knows that he is supposed to do his best in order to keep from being victimized; the criminal and the delinquent know that murder, rape, or shoplifting is prohibited. But they do not understand why. Yet, without this understanding the criminal and his victim can form only a phenomenalistic judgment whereby the world appears to operate without rhyme or reason and in an arbitrary manner that leaves them at its mercy.

The assumption that the criminal has more freedom of will, and uses illegitimate means to achieve blocked goals, and the victim, for the same reason, does not use the necessary care and self-protection or even precipitates the crime, do not provide a solution to the crime problem. Limitations on the freedom of will do not exclude goals and aspirations; moreover, aspiration belongs in functional roles if it is kept within the limits. All human beings have goals, not all of which can be achieved by any one person. Why have not all people, rather than only a fraction of them, turned to illegitimate alternatives? And why do not all people refrain from inviting crime and become victims of offenders?

Crime has existed since the dawn of history, and all crimes have been committed because of blocked aspirations, whatever their nature. They may be economic, intellectual, communal, sexual, or any other aspirations. Moreover, it may be said that the whole course of personality development, from infancy and early childhood to later life, has always been based primarily on learning to strive for certain cultural goals and learning to live with frustration if the goals are unattainable. This learning process and the frustrations that sometimes result have always been a necessary part of group membership. Even in the so-called primitive era of private vengeance and kin-revenge, the "offender" did not attack his victim only because of some innate drive toward violence. It was because the victim had something he wanted and could not obtain as easily in another way. Perhaps it was food, the skin of an animal, a special stone, or perhaps even the status that comes with power and success. In a certain sense, the criminal and delinquent have always been goal-oriented. The criminal of today is not basically different from the criminal of any other period of time. Only his aspirations and the limitations on his freedom of will have changed from time to time and from place to place, and these in accordance with the cultural definitions of the era and society in question. From this point of view, the status-seeking strivings of immature individuals, learned from and supported by their particular subcultures, can be understood only as a formal rejection of approved ways of achieving one's ambitions. Similarly, most studies today assume that the adolescent gang delinquent wants upward mobility in the normal middle-class fashion. This rather metaphysical approach to the allegedly class-conscious gang delinquent (with which viewpoint the public generally concurs) tries to measure delinquency and adolescence in terms of what these researchers think they should be and not in terms of what they actually are. And so the attempt is in vain. As has been suggested, this imaginary working-class boy "standing alone to face humiliation at the hands of middle-class agents is difficult to comprehend."[8] This approach stands up only if the ambition of the criminal or delinquent to challenge the middle-class system can be seen and interpreted as social gratification that his lack of any constructive ambition denies him. But this would presume that his will has been culturally saturated, but not limited. In other words he has an accurate picture of himself, his social environment, and the society's class system. However, to make this assumption is to contradict what we generally know about criminals and victims and what we primarily know about adolescents. The ability to perceive, learn, think, and reason in a culturally approved mature fashion cannot be effectively learned if one lives and functions in some isolated subculture in which he is not imbued with the values of the dominant culture and where its limitations on freedom of will cannot reach him.

Under these circumstances, it seems likely that for individuals such as criminals or delinquent gang adolescents inadequate socialization results in a lack of constructive ambitions or positive values. In other words, "rolelessness" may develop instead of "roleness." Because of his inadequate socialization and faulty aspiration-image, the criminal or the delinquent youth cannot determine which rights and duties are his. He cannot see his functional role, and so he cannot identify the constructive roles he would otherwise play.

Given this roleless state, the criminal or delinquent, unable to recognize the positive values expected of him, cannot form the positive aspirations expected of him. If the criminal or the delinquent youth turns to destructive ambitions, this is not so much a matter of choice among alternatives as an option available to him in the absence of a positive value system that is approved by the dominant power structure of the society.

The concept of the lower class versus the middle class and the predominant identification of the lower class with crime or delinquency make sense only if the middle class can be identified with the norm-forming social power. In no known human society or organized group are privileges and prohibitions evenly distributed, and the question of "whose ox is gored" depends for the most part on the ruling social power, as expressed by the law.

Although most prohibitions are set forth by the ruling social power in the form of law, their effectiveness is increased when reinforced by what might be called the informal, extralegal armament of the power structure—in the form of norms, bias, prejudice, and the like. Many studies of the crime problem seem to ignore this and to stress only the regulative structure of the law, both for criminals and victims. Indeed, the law, as the formal expression of the prevailing value system, is present in all its positive and negative aspects even before birth. It stays with the individual in every stage of his life. He is as much surrounded by it as by the air he breathes, and it follows him in all circumstances to the end of his life—and even after that. However, the law is not only coercive and negative in nature; it is also positive in that it affirms the values of the ruling social power. As such, it is not concerned always and exclusively with the realities of life: not what "is" but what "should be" is its central ideal.

All laws are formulated on the unspoken assumption that they are just, although they do not appear so to all members of a society, particularly to those who feel that they are more disadvantaged and enjoy fewer opportunities. One can ask, "Which human interests are worthy of being satisfied and . . . what is their proper order of rank? . . . The answer to these questions is a judgment of value."[9] The law serves the value system of the existing social power structure and enacts justice as interpreted by this system. As Hans Kelsen remarks, "Were it possible to answer the question of justice as we are able to solve problems of the technique of natural science or medicine, one would as little think of regulating the relations among men by positive law, that is by authoritative measure of coercion, as one thinks today of forceably prescribing by positive law how a steam engine should be built or a specific illness healed."[10]

The law consists of norms or rules of human behavior, but it is not only a regulative tool to simply prohibit crime and prescribe defense against lawbreaking. It is perhaps first of all a teleological instrument in the service of the existing social power structure. As such, the law is not concerned with universal reasons as to why particular types of behavior are required or prohibited, but it does try to achieve certain ends established by and related to the values of the social structure in power. In other words, whenever the law attempts to attain certain ends, at the same time it takes a position in favor of certain values and in so doing enables the society to distinguish between right and wrong. The values that the law supports are not the result of the law, but the reason for its existence. The law "presupposes (that one has) a mental picture of what (he) is doing and of why he is doing it,"[11] and in this way teaches the values created by the ruling power. If the criminal or the gang delinquent resorts to illegitimate alternatives, this means that he rejects the law's teachings because his lack of adequate socialization prevents him from understanding the teleological background of the norm.

Laws can be interpreted as right or wrong and argued accordingly, but they always represent what "should be." A demand for more or different opportunities for the criminal or delinquent, or for a reconciliation between the status of the middle-class boy and that of the lower-class delinquent, can be regarded as a hedonistic approach, but it cannot solve the basic issue of relativity of values. The fact that barriers exist for certain individuals or groups does not necessarily mean that the law is wrong, for it is right or wrong only in the way it interprets actions. The law makes objective rather than absolute judgments: objective because the judgments are regarded as "right" in terms of the prevailing and predominant norms and values. Whenever the criminal or delinquent breaks the law, this can be regarded as opposition only if he understands but disagrees with the lawmaking value system. In the case of efficient cultural saturation and adequate limitations on the free will, this could hardly happen. The fact that he understands and accepts the norm only as a regulation reveals his inadequate socialization.

Functional Responsibility of and for the Victim

The responsibility of the criminal for compensation or restitution to his victim, and the responsibility of the victim for his own victimization are not only problems of freedom of the will. Nor are they related only to the functional role of man in the particular society in which he lives. They are also involved in the puzzle of causality as posed by the law of the particular social structure in power. In fact, all these ideas are interrelated. "Perhaps the most troublesome of these lay words is the term, *to cause*."[12] What the traditional objective responsibility concept failed to see is the location of the causal nexus in a spectrum of crime in which the functional dynamics of lawbreaking processes can be viewed throughout their development. Lombroso's *uomo delinquente* became the curiosity of wax museums, and Ferri's "new horizons" stopped being a novelty long ago. But our present static understanding of responsibility and causality is a metaphorical option and had its beginnings centuries ago.

This does not mean that the other extreme is now proposed, although the general philosophical concept of an unlimited number of causes may not be distant from the concept of a limited free will. However, the *regressus in infinitum* of causes leads to conclusions that are just as absurd as acceptance of the principle of *post hoc ergo propter hoc,* which makes justice that is based on it doubtful.

The mother who gave birth to a murderer is one link in the chain of causes, but normally nobody would dream of charging her with a criminal contribution to the murder. At the same time, just because official statistical tables show that most juvenile delinquents come from the lower class, one cannot be suspicious of a young man simply because his father is a poverty-stricken shoeshiner. The imputation of law cannot be extended to the imputation of the facts.

The functional role of man sets the limit of the accountable links in the chain of causes, and his instrumentality is the cause-selecting factor for his responsibility. Crime is not only an individual act, but also a social phenomenon. Thus it is seen in the generative context of its participants, the criminal and the victim, as projected to their functional role. There is hardly any doubt that the crime-caused injury, harm, or other disadvantage of the victim was generated by the criminal and that the latter was thereby instrumental in curtailing the victim's performance of his role in society. The transposition of these "civil damages" into the body of its origin (that is, the criminal law) involves a complex of homogeneous full responsibility, wherein the criminal is called to account not only for violating the rules of his own societal responsibility, but also that he may restore his victim's potential functional responsibility. Also, it is far from true that all crimes "happen" to be committed; often the victim's negligence, precipitative action, or provocation contributes to the genesis or performance of a crime. The norm-delineated functional role of the victim is to do nothing to provoke others from attempting to injure his ability to play his role. At the same time, it expects him actively to prevent such attempts. This is the victim's functional responsibility. The extension of the formalistic and individualistic judgment of crime to an understanding of its dynamic course from a universal viewpoint reveals the complementary functional responsibilities of the victim and his criminal. And, this is where, within the field of criminology, "victimology" finds its place, and holds the promise of a better understanding of crime.

NOTES

1. Roscoe Pound, *An Introduction to the Philosophy of Law* (New Haven, 1965), p. 89.
2. With a few exceptions, such as Paul W. Tappan, *Crime, Justice and Correc-*

tion (New York, 1960), pp. 264–69; John Andenaes "Determinism and Criminal Law," *Journal of Criminal Law, Criminology and Police Science,* November-December 1956; the Detroit sociologist Father John E. Coogan (in the debate appearing in *Federal Probation* in 1952 and 1956); and others. Most writers on criminology do not try very hard to base their conceptual schemes on these indispensable foundations.

3. Morris Ginsberg, *On Justice in Society* (Harmondsworth, 1965), p. 168.

4. Heinrich Rickert, *System der Philosophie* (Tübingen, 1921), Vol. I, p. 254.

5. *Unaufgelöste Widerspruch,* in Georg Wilhelm Friedrich Hegel, *Encyclopädie der philosophischen Wissenschaften* (Leipzig, 1923), p. 209.

6. Franz Alexander and Hugo Staub, *The Criminal, the Judge, and the Public,* trans. Gregory Zilboorg (rev. ed., Glencoe, 1956), p. 127.

7. Jean-Paul Sartre, *Being and Nothingness,* trans. Hazel E. Barnes (New York, 1956), p. 555.

8. John I. Kitsuse and David C. Dietrick, "Delinquent Boys: A Critique," *American Sociological Review* (April 1959), p. 211.

9. Hans Kelsen, "The Metamorphoses of the Idea of Justice," in Paul Sayre, ed., *Interpretations of Modern Legal Philosophies Essays in Honor of Roscoe Pound* (New York, 1947), p. 392.

10. Ibid., p. 397.

11. Pound, *Introduction to the Philosophy of Law,* p. 25.

12. Wex S. Malone, "Nature of Proof of Cause-In-Fact," in Richard C. Donnelly, Joseph Goldstein, and Richard D. Schwartz, eds., *Criminal Law* (New York, 1962), p. 614.

Selected Bibliography

Abdou, Antoun Fahmy. *Le Consentement de la victime* (Paris, 1971).

Aeppli, Heinz. "Frauen als 'Opfer' vorgetäuschter Verbrechen," *Kriminalistik,* 1956, 10:215–16.

Amelunxen, Clemens. "Strafjustiz und Victimologie," *Kriminalistik,* 1969, 23:178–81.

———. *Das Opfer der Straftat* (Hamburg, 1970).

Amir, Menachem. "Victim Precipitated Forcible Rape," *Journal of Criminal Law, Criminology and Police Science,* 1967, 58:493–502.

———. *Patterns in Forcible Rape* (Chicago, 1971).

———. *Theoretical and Empirical Developments in Victimology* (in Hebrew, Jerusalem, 1973).

Amodio, E., P.V. Bondonio, U. Carnevali, G. Galli, V. Grevi, M. Pisani, and L. Rubini. *Vittime del delitto e solidarietá sociale* (Varese, 1975).

163

Anttila, Inkeri. "Compensation for Victims of Crime," *Revue Internationale de Droit Pénal,* 1973, 1–2:176–79.

Barrows, Samuel I. *The Sixth International Congress: Report of Its Proceedings and Conclusions* (Washington, D.C., 1903).

Becker, Pirmin. *Victimologische und präventive Aspekte in der Polizeilichen Kriminalstatistik* (Kriminalpolizeiant des Saarlandes).

Bentel, David J. "Selected Problems of Public Compensation to Victims of Crime," *Issues in Criminology,* 1968, 217–31.

Bernard, V.W. "Why People Become Victims of Medical Quackery," *American Journal of Public Health,* 1965, 55:1142–47.

Biderman, Albert A., Louise A. Johnson, Jenni McIntyre, and Adrianne W. Weir. *Report on a Pilot Study in the District of Columbia on Victimization and Attitudes Toward Law Enforcement* (Washington, D.C., 1967).

Blatt Burton. *Souls in Extremis: An Anthology on Victims and Victimizers* (Boston, 1973).

Block, M.K. and G.L. Long. "Subjective Probability of Victimization and Crime Levels," *Criminology,* 1973, 11:87–93.

Block, Richard, and Franklin E. Zimring. "Homicide in Chicago, 1965–1970," *Journal of Research in Crime and Delinquency,* 1973, 10:1–12.

Calewart, W., "La Victimologie et l'escroquerie," *Revue de Droit Pénal et de Criminologie,* 1959, 602–18.

Canepa, Giacomo, and T. Bandini. "The Personality of Incest Victims," *International Criminal Police Review,* 1967, 140–45.

Carrington, Frank G. *The Victims* (New Rochelle, N.Y., 1975).

Centre d'Etude de la Délinquance Juvénile, *Les enfants victimes de mauvais traitements* (Bruxelles, 1971).

Cherry, Richard R. *Lectures on the Growth of Criminal Law in Ancient Communities* (London, 1890).

Cornil, Paul. "Contribution de la 'victimologie' aux sciences criminologiques," *Revue de Droit Pénal et de Criminologie,* 1959, 587–600.

Curtis, Lynn A. "Victim Precipitation and Violent Crime," *Social Problems,* 1974, 21:594–605.

Dallaert, R. "Premiere confrontation de la psychologie criminelle et de la victimologie," *Revue de Droit Pénal et de Criminologie,* 1959, 628–34.

de Bray, L. "Quelques observations sur les victimes des délits de vol," *Revue de Droit Pénal et de Criminologie,* 1959, 643–49.

de Castro, Lola Aniyar. *La Victimologia* (Maracaibo, 1969).

DeCourcy, Peter and Judith. *A Silent Tragedy: Child Abuse in the Community* (Port Washington, N.Y., 1973).

Drapkin, Israel, and Emilio Viano, eds. *Victimology* (Lexington, Mass., 1974).

————. *Victimology: A New Focus* (Lexington, Mass., 1975), papers presented to the First International Symposium on Victimology, Jerusalem, 1973.

Duplissie, A.J. "Compensating Victims of Crimes of Violence," *International Police Review,* 1969, 24:8–10.

Edelhertz, Herbert, and Gilbert Geis. *Public Compensation to Victims of Crime* (New York, 1974).

Eglash, Albert. "Creative Restitution: Some Suggestions for Prison Rehabilitation Programs," *American Journal of Correction,* 1958, 20–34.

Ehrlich, Camillo. *Betrüger und ihre Opfer: Die Technik des Betrugs und seine Spezialisten* (Hamburg, 1969).

Eisenberg, Ulrich. "Zum Opferbereich in der Kriminologie," *Goltdammers Archiv für Strafrecht und Strafprocess,* 168–79, 1971.

Ellenberger, Henri. "Relations psychologiques entre le criminel et la victime," *Revue Internationale de Criminologie et de Police Technique,* 1954, 8:103–21.

Emerton, Ephraim. *Introduction to the History of the Middle Ages* (Ginn, 1888).

Ennis, Philip H. *Criminal Victimization in the United States: A Report of a National Survey* (Washington, D.C., 1967).

————. "Crime, Victims, and the Police," *Trans-action,* 1967, 36–44.

Fattah, Ezzat Abdel. "Quelques Problèmes posés à la justice pénale par la victimologie," *Annales Internationales de Criminologie,* 1966, 355–61.

————. *La victime est-elle coupable?* (Montreal, 1971).

Feeney, Dean T.G. "Compensation for the Victims of Crime," *Canadian Journal of Corrections,* 1968, 10:261–71.

Fogel, D., Burt Galaway, and Joe Hudson. "Restitution in Criminal Justice: a Minnesota Experiment," *Criminal Law Bulletin,* 1972, 8:681–91.

Fox, S.S., and D.J. Scherl. "Crisis Intervention with Victims of Rape," *Social Work,* 1972, 37–42.

Fry, Margery. *Arms of the Law* (London, 1951).

————. "Justice for Victims," *The Observer* London, July 7, 1957.

Gasser, Rudolf. *Victimologie: Kritische Betrachtungen zu einem neuen kriminologischen Begriff* (dissert., Zürich, 1965).

Geisler, Erika. *Das sexuell missbrauchte Kind: Beitrag zur sexuellen Entwicklung, ihrer Gefährdung und zu forensischen Fragen* (Göttingen, 1959).

Gibbens, T.C.N., and Joyce Prince. *Child Victims of Sex Offenses* (London, 1963).

Goll, August. *Verbrecher bei Shakespeare,* German trans. Oswald Gerloff (Stuttgart, c. 1908).

Heinz, Wolfgang. *Bestimmungsgründe der Anzeigebereitschaft des Opfers: Ein kriminologischer Beitrag zum Problem der differentiellen Wahrscheinlichkeit strafrechtlicher Sanktionierung* (dissert., Freiburg i. Br., 1972).

Helfer, Ray E., and C. Henry Kempe, eds. *The Battered Child* (3rd ed., Chicago, 1969).

Hemard, J. "Le consentement de la victime dans le délit de coups et blessures," *Revue Critique de Legislation et de Jurisprudence,* 1939, 24:293–319.

————. "Lehren der Statistik," *Köllner Zeitung,* 447, Sept. 4, 1934.

————. *Punishment, Its Origin, Purpose and Psychology* (London, 1937).

Hentig, Hans von. *The Criminal and His Victim: Studies in the Sociobiology of Crime* (New Haven, 1948).

————. *Das Verbrechen,* Vol. II: *Der Delinquent im Griff der Umwältkräfte* (Berlin, 1962).

Hepburn, John, and Harwin L. Voss. "Patterns of Criminal Homicide: A Comparison of Chicago and Philadelphia," *Criminology,* 1970, 8:21–45.

Hess, Albert. *Die Kinderschädung unter besonderer Berücksichtigung der Tatsituation* (Leipzig, 1934).

Hogan, B. "Victims as Parties to Crime," *Criminal Law Review,* 1962, 683–95.

Hudson, Joe, and Burt Galaway, eds. *Considering the Victim: Readings in Restitution and Victim Compensation* (Springfield, Ill., 1975).

Jacobsen, Chanoch. "The Permissive Society and Its Victims: A Preliminary Statement," *International Journal of Criminology and Penology,* 1974, 2:173–79.

Johnston, Stanley W. "Toward a Supra-national Criminology," *International Journal of Criminology and Penology,* 1974, 2:133–47.

Kaiser, Günther. "Das Kind als Opfer," *Kriminalistik,* 1970, 24:122–26.

———. *Kriminologie: Eine Einführung in die Grundlagen* (2nd ed., Karlsruhe, 1973).

Kaiser, Günther, Fritz Sack, and Hartmut Schellhoss. *Kleines Kriminologisches Wörterbuch* (Freiburg i.B., 1974).

Lamborn, LeRoy. "Toward a Victim Orientation in Criminal Theory," *Rutger's Law Review,* 1968, 22:733–68.

Landau, Simha F., Israel Drapkin, and Shlomo Arad. "Homicide Victims and Offenders: An Israeli Study," *The Journal of Criminal Law and Criminology,* 1974, 65:390–96.

Lefkowitz, Bernard, and Kenneth G. Gross. *The Victims: The Wylie-Hoffert Murder Case and Its Strange Aftermath* (New York, 1969).

Lempp, Reinhart. "Seelische Schädigung von Kindern als Opfer von gewaltlosen Sittlichkeitsdelikten, *Neue Juristische Wochenschrift,* 1968, 2265–68.

Lernell, Leszek. *The Fundamentals of General Criminology* (in Polish, Warsaw, 1973).

Linden, A.M. "Victims of Crime and Tort Law," *Canadian Bar Journal,* 1969, 17–33.

———. "International Conference on Compensation to Innocent Victims of Violent Crime," *Criminal Law Quarterly,* 1969, 145–49.

MacDonald, John M. *The Murderer and His Victim* (Springfield, Ill., 1961).

———. *Rape Offenders and Their Victims* (Springfield, Ill., 1971).

Mack, J.A. "A Victim-Role Typology of Rational-Economic Property Crime," *International Journal of Criminology and Penology,* 1974, 2:149–58.

Makarewicz, J. *Einführung in die Philosophie des Strafrechts auf entwicklungsgeschichtlicher Grundlage* (Stuttgart, 1906).

Marcuse, Max. "Männer als Opfer von Kindern," *Archiv für Kriminalanthropologie und Kriminalistik,* 1914, 56:188–92.

McGrath, W.T. "Compensation to Victims of Crime in Canada," *Canadian Journal of Corrections,* 1970, 12:11–24.

Matthes, Ilse. *Minder jährige "Geschädigte" als Zeugen in Sittlichkeits Prozessen* (Wiesbaden, 1961).

Mäkinen, Tuija. *Rikosvahinkojen Korvaukset* (Compensation for Crime Damages, in Finnish, Helsinki, 1975).

Mendelsohn, Beniamin. "Une nouvelle branche de la science bio-psycho-sociale: la victimologie," *Revue Internationale de Criminologie et de Police Technique*, 1956, 10:95–109.

————. "La victimologie: science actuelle," *Revue de Droit Pénal et de Criminologie*, 1959, 619–27.

————. "The Origin of the Doctrine of Victimology," *Excerpta Criminologica*, 1963, 3:239–44.

————. "Le Rapport entre la victimologie et la problème du génocide: pour un code de prévention du génocide," *Etudes Internationales de Psycho-Sociologie Criminelle*, 1968, 14:14–53.

Miyazawa, Koichi. *Fundamentals of Victimology* (in Japanese, Tokyo, 1966).

————. *Victimology* (in Japanese, Tokyo, 1967).

Miyazawa, Koichi, ed., *The Crime and the Victim: Victimology in Japan* (in Japanese, Tokyo, 1974).

Myers, S.A. "The Child Slayer: a 25-year Survey of Homicides Involving Preadolescent Victims," *Archives of General Psychiatry*, 1967, 17:211–13.

Nagel, Willem H. "The Notion of Victimology in Criminology," *Excerpta Criminologica*, 1963, 3:245–47.

————. "Structural Victimization," *International Journal of Criminology and Penology*, 1974, 2:99–132.

Nagy Teréz and Ervin Cséka. "L'indemnisation des victimes de l'infraction pénale," *Revue Internationale de Droit Pénal*, 1973, 1–2:180–88.

Ortloff, Herman. *Der Adhäsionsprozess* (Leipzig, 1864).

Paasch, Fritz R. *Grundprobleme der Victimologie* (dissert., Münster, 1965).

Paris Prison Congress, 1895. *Summary Report* (London).

Pećar, J. "The Role of Victims in Homicide in Slovakia" (in Slovenian) *Revija za Kriminalistiko in Kriminologijo*, 1971, 22:258–65.

Pollock, Frederick, and Frederic William Maitland. *The History of English Law* (2nd ed., Cambridge, 1898).

President's Commission on Law Enforcement and Administration of Justice. *The Challenge of Crime in a Free Society*, and *Task Force Report: Crime and Its Impact, An Assessment* (Washington, D.C., 1967).

Quinney, Richard. "Who is the Victim?" *Criminology*, 1972, 10:314–23.

Raffalli, Henri Christian. "The Battered Child, An Overview of a Medical, Legal, and Social Problem," *Crime and Delinquency,* 1970, 16:139–50.

Ranjeva, H., L. Gayral, P. Moron, and P. Fray. "La notion de victime latente, contribution psychopathologique à l'étude de la victimologie," *Annales Mèdico-Psychologiques,* 1971, 349–66.

Rehfeldt, Bernhard. *Die Wurzehn des Rechtes* (Berlin, 1951).

Reinhardt, Heinz. *Die Bestrafung der Unzucht mit Kindern unter besonderer Berücksichtigung des Verhaltens und der Persönlichkeit des Opfers* (Bern, 1967).

Roesner, Ernst. "Mörder und ihre Opfer," *Monatschrift für Kriminologie und Strafrechtsreform,* 1938, 29:209–28.

Ruggles-Brise, E. *Report to the Secretary of State for the Home Department on the Proceedings of the Fifth and Sixth International Penitentiary Congresses* (London, 1901).

Ryan, William. *Blaming the Victim* (New York, 1971).

Schafer, Stephen. *Restitution to Victims of Crime* (London, 1960).

———. *Compensation and Restitution to Victims of Crime* (2nd ed., Montclair, N.J., 1970).

———. *The Victim and His Criminal: A Study in Functional Responsibility* (New York, 1968).

———. "Compensation of Victims of Criminal Offenses," *Revue Internationale de Droit Pénal,* 1973, 1–2:105–75.

———. "The Proper Role of a Victim-Compensation System," *Crime and Delinquency,* 1975, 21:45–49.

———. *Introduction to Criminology* (Reston, Virginia, 1976).

Schafer, Stephen, Mary S. Knudten, and Richard D. Knudten, *Social Problems in a Changing Society: Issues and Deviances* (Reston, Virginia, 1975).

Schneider, Hans Joachim. "Der Pädophile Straftäter und sein Opfer," *Monatschrift für Kriminologie und Strafrechtsreform,* 1965, 48:91–94.

———. *Kriminologie: Wissenschaft vom Verbrechensopfer* (Täbingen, 1975).

Schoreit, Armin. *Entschädigung der Verbrechensopfer als öffentliche Aufgabe* (Berlin, 1973).

Schorsch, Eberhard. *Sexualstraftäter* (Stuttgart, 1971).

Schönke, Adolf. *Beiträge zur Lehre vom Adhäsionsprozess* (Berlin, 1935).

Schüler-Springorum, Horst. "Uber Victimologie," *Festschrift für Richard M. Honig* (Göttingen, 1970), 201–15.

Schultz, Hans. "Kriminologische und strafrechtliche Bemerkungen zur Beziehung zwischen Täter und Opfer," *Schweizerische Zeitschrift für Strafrecht,* 1956, 171–92.

Sellin, Thorsten, and Marvin E. Wolfgang. *The Measurement of Delinquency* (New York, 1964).

Serwe, L.H. "Täter-Opfer-Beziehungen bei einigen Sittlichkeitsdelikten *Kriminalistik,* 1970, 24:73–75.

Sethna, Minocher J. *Society and the Criminal* (Bombay, 1952), *Jurisprudence* (Girgaon-Bombay, 1959).

Simon, J. "Le consentement de la victime justifie-t-il le lésions corporelles?" *Revue de Droit Pénal et Criminologie,* 1933, 13:457–76.

Smigel, Erwin O. "Public Attitudes Toward Stealing as Related to the Size of the Victim Organization," *American Sociological Review,* 1956, 21:320–27.

Smigel, Erwin O., and Laurence H. Ross, eds., *Crimes Against Bureaucracy* (New York, 1970).

Smith, Kathleen J. *A Cure for Crime: The Case for the Self-Determinate Prison Sentence* (London, 1965).

Stamm, Judith. *Das sexuell geschädigte Kind in der Strafuntersuchung* (Zürich, 1967).

Starke, Wolfgang. *Die Entschädigung des Verletzten* (Freiburg, 1959).

Stockert, F.G., ed. *Das sexuell gefährdete Kind* (Stuttgart, 1965).

Stokols, D., and E. Schopler. "Reactions to Victims under Conditions of Situational Detachment, The Effects of Responsibility, Severity and Expected Future Interaction," *Journal of Personality and Social Psychology,* 1973, 25:199–209.

Stolk, Mary van. *The Battered Child in Canada* (Toronto, 1972).

Sutherland, Sandra and Donald J. Scherl. "Patterns of Response Among Victims of Rape," *American Journal of Orthopsychiatry,* 1970, 40:503–11.

"Symposium: Compensation to Victims of Crimes of Personal Violence, An Examination of the Scope of the Problem." *Minnesota Law Review,* 1965, 50:211–310.

"Symposium: Governmental Compensation for Victims of Violence." *Southern California Law Review,* 1970, 43:1–121.

Tahon, R. "Le consentement de la victime," *Revue de Droit Pénal et de Criminologie,* 1952, 321–42.

Tallack, William. *Reparation to the Injured, and the Rights of the Victims of Crime to Compensation* (London, 1900).

Tormes, Y.M. *Child Victims of Incest* (Washington, D.C., 1968).

Trube-Becker, Elisabeth. *Frauen als Mörder* (München, 1974).

Ueno, S., and I. Ishiyama. "Ein Beitrag über die Analyse von Opfertypen; die statistische Analyse der 5,340 Obduktionsfälle aus der Universität Tokyo," *Deutsche Zeitschrift für die gesamte gerichtliche Medizin,* 1962, 53:55–71.

Victims of Crime. U.S. Senate Hearings (Washington, D.C., 1972) and Report (Washington, D.C., 1973).

Waeckerling, Carlo. *Die Sorge für den Verletzten im Strafrecht* (Zürich, 1946).

Weis, Kurt. " 'Victimologie' und 'Victorologie' in der Kriminologie," *Monatschrift für Kriminologie und Strafrechtsreform,* 1972, 55:170–80.

Werfel, Franz. *Nicht der Mörder, der Ermordete ist schuldig* (München, 1920).

Wolf, Eric. *Vom Wesen des Täters* (Berlin, 1932).

Wolfgang, Marvin E. *Patterns in Criminal Homicide* (Philadelphia, 1958).

————. "Analytical Categories for Research and Theory on Victimization," in Armand Mergen-Herbert Schäfer, ed., *Kriminologische Wegzeichen* (Hamburg, 1967), 169–85.

Wolfgang, Marvin E., ed. *Crime and Race: Conceptions and Misconceptions* (New York, 1970).

Wood, Pamela Lakes. "The Victim in a Forcible Rape Case: A Feminist View," *The American Criminal Law Review,* 1973, 11:345–47.

Woods, G.D. "Some Aspects of Pack Rape in Sydney," *Australian and New Zealand Journal of Criminology,* 1969, 2:105–19.

Zipf, Heinz. "Die Bedeutung der Viktimologie für die Strafrechtspflege," *Monatschrift für Kriminologie und Strafrechtsreform,* 1970, 53:1–13.

Index